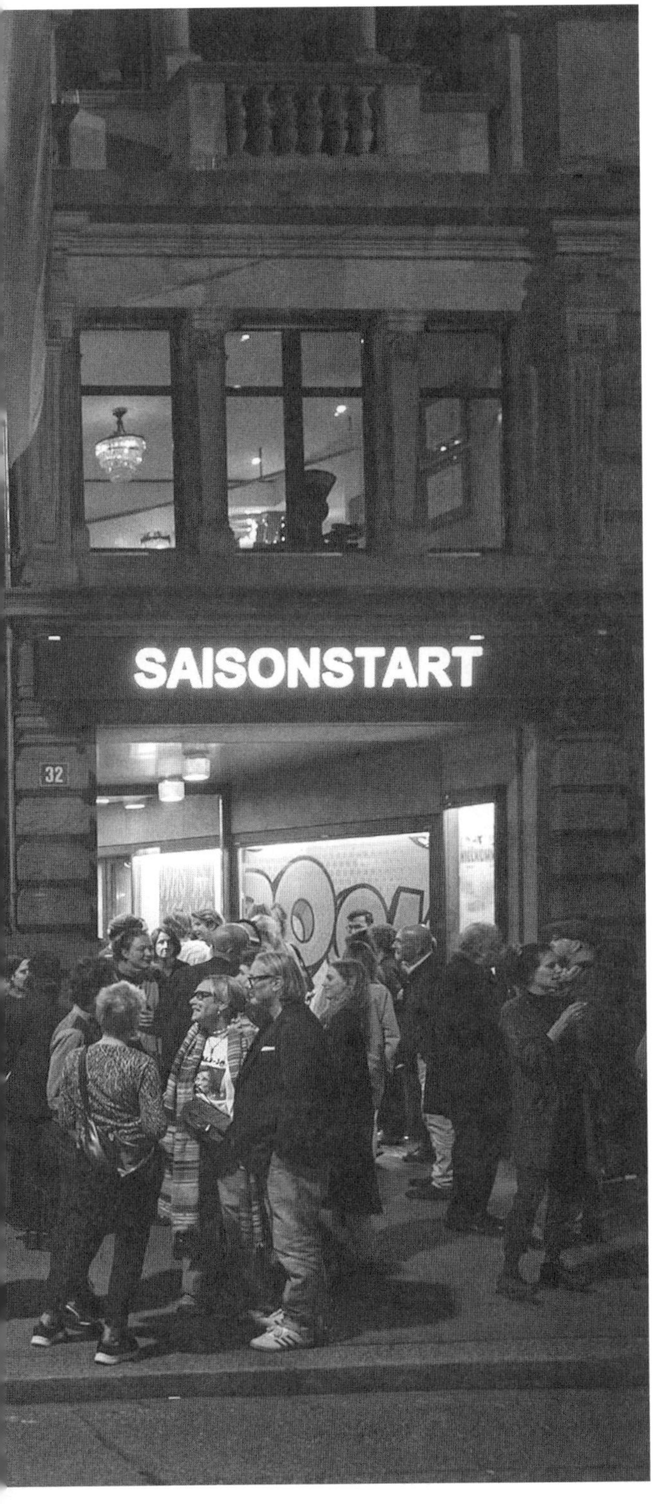

Theater

VOLUME 55, NUMBER 2

TOM SELLAR, *Editor*

DAVID GEFFEN SCHOOL OF DRAMA AT YALE

YALE REPERTORY THEATRE

EDITOR   Tom Sellar

GUEST EDITORS, *Institutional Dramaturgies*   Lily Climenhaga and Noah Lena Vercauteren

ASSOCIATE EDITOR   Gabrielle Hoyt

MANAGING EDITORS   Daria Kerschenbaum and Georgia Petersen

ADVISORY BOARD   James Bundy, Florie Seery, and Catherine Sheehy

CONTRIBUTING EDITORS   Una Chaudhuri, Thomas F. DeFrantz, Liz Diamond, Miriam Felton-Dansky, Jacob Gallagher-Ross, Eric M. Glover, Gitta Honegger, Shannon Jackson, Kimberly Jannarone, Jonathan Kalb, Renate Klett, Jennifer Krasinski, James Leverett, Mark Lord, Charles McNulty, Tavia Nyong'o, Katherine Profeta, Joseph Roach, Marc Robinson, Chantal Rodriguez, Daniel Sack, Alisa Solomon, Andrea Tompa, Paul Walsh

Theater is published three times a year (February, May, and November) by Duke University Press, 905 W. Main St., Suite 18B, Durham, NC 27701, on behalf of the David Geffen School of Drama at Yale/Yale Repertory Theatre. For a list of the sources in which *Theater* is indexed and abstracted, see dukeupress.edu/theater.

SUBMISSIONS AND
EDITORIAL CORRESPONDENCE
See the Duke University Press *Theater* website for detailed submission guidelines: read.dukeupress.edu/theater. Send manuscripts for submission and letters concerning editorial matters to *Theater*, PO BOX 208244, New Haven, CT 06520-8244; theater.magazine @yale.edu.

PERMISSIONS
Photocopies for course or research use that are supplied to the end user at no cost may be made without explicit permission or fee. Photocopies that are provided to the end user for a fee may not be made without payment of permission fees to Duke University Press. Send requests for permission to republish copyrighted material to permissions @dukeupress.edu.

WORLD WIDE WEB
Visit the journal's website at theatermagazine.org and Duke University Press at dukeupress.edu.

SUBSCRIPTIONS
Direct all orders to Duke University Press, Journals Customer Relations, 905 W. Main St., Suite 18B, Durham, NC 27701. Annual subscription rates: print-plus-electronic institutions, $328; print-only institutions, $312; e-only institutions, $247; e-only individuals, $15; individuals, $30; students, $20. For information on subscriptions to the e-Duke Journals Scholarly Collections, contact dup_libraryrelations@duke.edu. Print subscriptions: add $11 postage and applicable HST (including 5% GST) for Canada; add $14 postage outside the US and Canada. Back volumes (institutions): $312. Single issues: institutions, $104; individuals, $14. For more information, contact Duke University Press Journals at 888-651-0122 (toll-free in the US and Canada) or at 919-688-5134; subscriptions @dukeupress.edu.

ADVERTISEMENTS
Direct inquiries about advertising to Journals Advertising Coordinator, journals_advertising@dukeupress.edu.

© 2025 by David Geffen School of Drama at Yale/ Yale Repertory Theatre
ISSN 0161-0775

CONTRIBUTORS

MARIANA ARISTIZÁBAL is a Latinx theater-maker with vast experience in collaborative and devising methodologies. Her work expands from directing and performing to community and audience development and facilitating. She has led projects nationally and internationally. She is currently associate director at Company Three and codirector of award-winning company MarianaMalena. She has worked for theaters such as the Royal Shakespeare Company, Royal Court, Young Vic, Old Vic, Donmar Warehouse, Chipping Norton, and Blue Elephant, among others.

KEITH BARKER is the director of the Foerster Bernstein New Play Development Program at the Stratford Festival, and former artistic director at Native Earth Performing Arts in Toronto. In 2023 Keith was a recipient of the Johanna Metcalf Prize; in 2020 he received a Dora Mavor Award for Outstanding New Play and the Playwrights Guild of Canada's Carol Bolt Award. Keith was a finalist for the Governor General's Literary Award for Drama in 2018.

JULIAN BLAUE is a German Norwegian performance artist. He performs at prestigious venues including Staatsoper Berlin, Volksbühne Berlin, Det Norske Teatret, and the Rio Art Museum. Blaue is part of the duo Blaue & Poppy (*The Trial against Ourselves*, 2021) and a staging of Edy Poppy's novel *Iggy*.

PETER M. BOENISCH, originally from Munich, is professor of dramaturgy at Aarhus University (Denmark). His research areas are theater direction, dramaturgy, and the institutional conditions of theater production in twenty-first-century European theater. At Aarhus he is director of the research program "Cultural Transformations."

MAIRI BRASCOUPÉ is a multidisciplinary Algonquin (Kitigan Zibi First Nation) artist and producer from unceded Algonquin Territory, Ottawa. She combines traditional and contemporary techniques, highlighting land-based learning and intergenerational knowledge sharing. With a bachelor of design from Ryerson University and a master's from Central Saint Martins, she emphasizes decolonizing design. As the Cultural Resident for Indigenous Theatre at the National Arts Centre, she produces community and education programming to foster understanding and make the NAC more inclusive for Indigenous communities.

LILY CLIMENHAGA is a FWO postdoctoral fellow at Ghent University completing the project "Institutionalized Resistance: Milo Rau's NTGent Period." Lily is also a dramaturg, translator, critic, blogger, editor, and occasional stage manager.

YUVVIKI DIOH has been working as a diversity agent at the Schauspielhaus Zürich since February 2022, coshaping the institution's diversity-oriented organizational development. Yuvviki works on antiracist, queer-feminist, and power- and socio-critical topics. She has held various roles and functions (acting, creative consultant, production management, association management) in the independent theater scene in Zurich.

MARTA KEIL is a performing arts dramaturg and researcher currently based in Utrecht. Her research focuses on institutional critique, exhaustion, and withdrawal. She collaborates as dramaturg and curator with various European institutions and artists, and works as tutor at DAS Theatre, Academy for Theatre and Dance, Amsterdam University of the Arts.

CHRISTINE KORTE is currently on faculty at NYU Berlin teaching courses in German theater history and German cinema, as well as within the Tisch BFA Acting Program, "Stanislavsky, Brecht and Beyond." Christine completed her PhD on the Berliner Volksbühne under Frank Castorf and is currently pursuing postdoctoral research at the Freie Universität Berlin on diversification initiatives underway in Berlin's major theater institutions.

KOPANO MAROGA (they/them) is a South African performance artist, writer, educator, and cultural worker. Their debut poetry collection, *Jesus Thesis and Other Critical Fabulations*, was released in 2020 and later, in 2023, translated into German. Their writing has been published in *ArtThrob*, *The Mail*, *The Guardian*, *Indent: The Body and the Performative*, *rekto:verso*, *Contemporary And*, and elsewhere.

OLGA MOUAK is a French actress, performer, and writer based in Paris. She entered the National School of Performing Arts in Montpellier, graduating in 2016. She has since worked with directors such as Angélica Liddell, Milo Rau, and Bob Wilson, honing her talents on stages across multiple European countries. Alongside French Malian author and director Eva Doumbia, Olga has been participating in theater projects centered around stories that so far remained untold on French stages.

MŪKONZI MŪSYOKI is a theater scholar, playwright, and dramaturg. He is currently a PhD candidate at the University of Alberta in Theatre and Performance Studies. He has worked with different theaters across Canada, Kenya, and Uganda. Mūkonzi works as a dramaturg for new play development at the Stratford Festival.

NELDA MURAY PRADO is an actress, director, and teacher trained at the University of Chile and one of the founders of Agrupación Cultural La Dramática Nacional. Her artistic work focuses on the tradition and social history of Chile. She recently published *Recabarren, Historical Drama*, coauthored with historian Gabriel Salazar.

UGORAN PRASAD is an associate artistic director at the Garasi Performance Institute in Yogyakarta. He earned a PhD in theater and performance from the Graduate Center of the City University of New York.

MILO RAU is the artistic director of the Vienna Festival / Wiener Festwochen. Rau studied sociology and German and Romance languages and literature in Paris, Berlin, and Zurich with Pierre Bourdieu and Tzvetan Todorov, among others. Since 2002, he has published over fifty plays, films, books, and actions.

TOM SELLAR is editor of *Theater* and professor in the practice of Dramaturgy and Dramatic Criticism at the David Geffen School of Drama at Yale University.

MARCOS DAVI SILVA STEUERNAGEL is an assistant professor of theater at the New School who writes on performance and politics in Brazil and across the Americas. With Diana Taylor, he coedited *What Is Performance Studies?* (2015) and *Resistant Strategies* (2021), and he has published in *TDR*, *Latin American Theatre Review*, and the *Journal of Global South Studies*.

JUDY VANDEN THOREN is a Belgian-born and -based cultural worker, coach, and DEI expert. She graduated as an anthropologist in 2002 and subsequently worked mainly in the nonprofit sector, in various positions. She tried to make organizations inclusive from within but decided to do so as an external facilitator in 2017. Now she works mainly with cultural houses and nongovernmental organizations.

NOAH LENA VERCAUTEREN (they/them) is a writer, editor, dramaturg, and PhD researcher affiliated at the University of Ghent, Belgium, and the University of Amsterdam, the Netherlands. Their research focuses on the positions and practices of institutional dramaturgs at Flemish and Dutch city theaters.

ANNA VOLKLAND is a freelance theater scholar in Berlin. A graduate dramaturg in theater, performance, and dance, she began her research in 2014 on the "forgotten" history of state and city theaters in the former German Democratic Republic (East Germany) and Federal Republic of Germany (West Germany), focusing on the attempts of theater-makers to (radically) "democratize" theater institutions since the late 1960s. She was a research assistant at the Berlin University of the Arts (2014–20).

CONTENTS

Title Page: Exterior of
Schauspielhaus Zürich,
Zurich, Switzerland, 2024.
Photo: Laura Kaufmann

Inside Back Cover:
Milo Rau's *Compassion,
the Story of the Machine
Gun,* NTGent, Gent,
Belgium, 2018. Photo:
Michiel Devijver

Up Front

INSTITUTIONAL REPAIR: THE LONG PATH AHEAD

TOM SELLAR

Devastating political news came as we finished this issue on institutional values, as the us election in November 2024 brought sweeping, unchecked powers to a right wing inflected by xenophobic extremism. Among the promises made by the campaigns' victors: prosecution of political enemies; use of military force against protesters; deportation of vulnerable immigrants; and politicization, hobbling, and outright elimination of federal agencies.

The unambiguous election outcome is bad news for artistic organizations as well as gut-wrenching to all who abhor this vision and wonder how a voting majority could ever have come to embrace it. One explanation might lie in the profound distrust that most Americans—like voters all over the world since the 2008 financial crisis and the 2020 pandemic—now have for institutions and the elites who run them. In an era of economic inequality, sharp rises in the cost of living, and seemingly endless wars for distant causes, the lack of confidence comes from more than one ideology. The left contests legacies of colonialism and points to institutions as instruments of inequality and oppression. On the right, a different form of frustration with the status quo has given rise to fervent antisystem populism, marked by contempt for the political and cultural establishment.

In the cultural sphere, theaters now sit uncomfortably between these camps— they are semipublic nonprofits in the United States and often subsidized entities abroad. To move forward, us institutions, like their global counterparts, will need to defend their missions and accomplishments while also reinventing themselves as accountable to their publics and essential for their communities.

While the work of diversity, equity, and inclusion has altered the American theater in recent years, circumstances and strategies of theaters outside the United States are rarely considered. North Americans might start by looking at those theaters. This issue of *Theater* assembles international scholars and artistic professionals to consider

Theater 55:2   DOI 10.1215/01610775-11683455

Former AfD party member Frauke Petry speaks at the Wiener Prozess (Vienna Trials) as her husband and fellow former AfD member, Marcus Pretzell, looks on. Wiener Festwochen, Vienna, Austria, 2024. Photo: Inés Baucher

how theaters are critically refining their own institutional values and identities—or how they should. The articles included here do not offer a comprehensive or composite picture: in particular, we hope to hear more from theater institutions in Asia, Australia, and Oceania in the future. But these collected voices articulate changes already underway as well as needs and aspirations for the fast-approaching future.

Navigating the dizzying social, political, and technological changes of the past decade, and the years since 2020 in particular, theaters have found themselves in unexpected terrain. Once these institutions—especially in countries with traditions of public culture and state subsidy—thought of themselves as civic forums. As recently as a decade ago, the stage and the dialogue arising from it contributed to a kind of town square. Productions, programs, and appointments of theater leaders might be debated in newspapers or broadcast media: a lively arena, but largely a manageable one with known boundaries. Public perceptions and commentary today form on social media, where theaters find themselves managing essential dimensions of their institutional identities online, in posts and public statements, and in response to others. In another era—say, that of the postwar "director's theater"—audiences might have looked to the stage for artists' metaphorical reflections on society, history, and current events. Today they expect to hear directly from theater organizations, and in other forms: artistic leaders must defend their programming, policies, and appointments of senior leadership, and those who dare to undertake any platforming of controversial viewpoints must then justify that choice.

How do internal reorientations for diversity and equity play out in the new sphere of online commentary and image? And how are these contexts shaping (or deriving from) the defining critical values of theater organizations—the "dramaturgy" component in institutional dramaturgy? Do creative structures for collaboration, discovered in the studio, successfully transfer to the institution, where managerial values have long reigned? Will theaters choose the path of remaking themselves and reorganizing producing structures to emphasize equity, care, inclusion, and decolonization? Or is that just for artists—while a business-as-usual administrative and producing structure remains intact, evading transparency while concentrating the values making in the hands of a select few? Such questions were successfully raised, if not definitively answered, at the 2024 Wiener Festwochen curated by Milo Rau, resulting in a new charter for the festival cocreated with the citizens of Vienna. We have included it with Rau's introduction as a possible example of change. For we need templates for transformation just as we need institutions to succeed.

Special thanks to guest coeditors Lily Climenhaga and Noah Lena Vercauteren for their inspired vision, and to all the contributors who shared their time and ideas.

The exterior of
Koninklijke Vlaamse
Schouwburg (KVS),
Brussels, Belgium,
2013. Courtesy of KVS

LILY CLIMENHAGA AND CHRISTINE KORTE

CREATING VAGRANT INSTITUTIONS FOR A MULTIPERSPECTIVE WORLD

I.

Since 2015, Berlin's Volksbühne has been in near-constant crisis. Built in 1913, the Volksbühne is a dissident institution in the cultural landscape of the German capital. In 1992, controversial East German director Frank Castorf was named artistic director of the institution, given three years by the freshly unified Berlin Senate to become "famous or dead."[1] In March 2015, it was announced that after twenty-five years Castorf would depart the theater. Artistic directors' tenures mostly end without much fanfare, but for Berlin, Castorf was the Volksbühne and the Volksbühne was Berlin.[2] On April 22, 2015, it was announced that Belgian curator Chris Dercon would replace Castorf.[3] However, Dercon's gentrified, international, decentralized vision for the theater was incompatible with Castorf's Volksbühne as the rebel spirit of untamable East Berlin.[4] During Dercon's (much-discussed) disastrous 255 days, open letters were penned by Volksbühne employees and the public alike; the theater was occupied day and night for six days by Dust to Glitter, a group that dreamed of collective leadership; an actor dumped beer on the minister of cultural affairs; feces were left at Dercon's office door; and he was put under police protection.[5] In April 2018, Dercon announced his departure, and a year later director René Pollesch (a Volksbühne staple since 2001) was named incoming artistic director for 2021/2022. Klaus Dörr became interim artistic director in 2018, a period first disrupted by pandemic shutdowns in March 2020 and again when Dörr was abruptly dismissed in March 2021 following #MeToo allegations.[6] Pollesch launched his opening season in the lull of the pandemic, seeming to mark the end of six years of institutional crisis, but critics still grumbled: Pollesch was directing at other theaters, too much Pollesch, too few classics, too few spectators, and too much reclamation and not enough innovation.[7] Then, on February 26, 2024, at age sixty-one, Pollesch suddenly died. Reeling from the loss, the theater began yet another leadership search.

Theater 55:2 DOI 10.1215/01610775-11683468
© 2025 by Lily Climenhaga and Christine Korte

On October 4, 2024, it was announced that Vergard Vinge and Ida Müller of Vinge/Müller would be interim artistic directors, but the duo turned down the position amid cuts to Berlin's cultural subsidies. On February 7, 2025, former Volksbühne dramaturg Matthias Lilienthal was officially named the new artistic director, to be accompanied by Florentina Holzinger and Marlene Monteiro Freitas as artistic board.[8]

This decade-long crisis is emblematic of how an institution's success is determined not merely by what appears onstage but also in its complicated positioning with regard to political interests, community expectations, and societal shifts. It is indicative of how cultural decisions—spaces that engage social and political movements in aesthetic and representational terms—are themselves part of public discourse: driven by interrelated public demands, media speculation, and political motives. The Volksbühne's future lies in an exceedingly complex negotiation of culture, politics, public, and history in creating an institutional identity that can overcome the one curated by Castorf that, ten years later, has not yielded to a parade of successors. So, what will the Volksbühne be in three years? Famous, dead, or—as Castorf threatened should the institution become irrelevant—a swimming pool?[9]

Wunderbaum's *Die Hundekot-Attacke*, Theaterhaus Jena, Jena, Germany, 2023. Photo: Joachim Dette

II.

In 1767, German playwright and critic Gotthold Ephraim Lessing took up an appointment at Hamburg's newly formed—but short-lived—National Theater (1767–69). Here, under the official title of "legal adviser," though often credited as the first dramaturg, Lessing held an institutional role. He was actively employed by and for the theater as a critic and commentator.[10] The most significant document to emerge from the playwright's time with the theater was *The Hamburg Dramaturgy*, a series of texts that sought to "develop a more rigorous, objective and analytical theater discourse and practice."[11] In the 101 short essays that make up *The Hamburg Dramaturgy*, Lessing underscores the importance of the national theater in developing a theater for the nation: performing a national canon of plays in the language and style of the audience in a historical moment where there was no united sense of national self. The theater became a discursive, legitimizing element in the construction of national-cultural identities for a new class of people with enough free time and disposable income to recreationally attend theater.[12] Lessing—alongside reflections on acting—called for the development of a new canon of plays that were socially and culturally relevant for its audiences, dramas that spoke to the lives and experiences of ordinary people "whose circumstances resemble our [this bourgeois audiences'] own."[13] Lessing's time at Hamburg—while largely outside the realm of production—highlights the dynamic role theater institutions play, representing the complexity of contemporary society (with all its conflicts and contradictions), while participating in the same social, political, and cultural discussions presented on their stages.[14] Zooming out from Hamburg, these are institutions that have in various historical and cultural contexts constructed seemingly unified, singular, and fixed identities—even if local and global realities are none of these things.

Dramaturgs have been given many different titles depending on their institutional, national, and historical context: artistic associate, literary manager, development dramaturg, production dramaturg, institutional dramaturg. Regardless of title, dramaturgy, since Lessing, has been a public-oriented practice. The dramaturg is an interlocutor between production and spectator, and institution and audience.[15] Slovenian dramaturg Eda Čufer, in her fifteen theses on the dramaturg's role, identifies dramaturgy as an intermediation between three autonomous spheres: (1) philosophy, theory, and academic discourse; (2) literary and theory practice; and (3) theater as an institution of public significance and ideological discourse.[16]

The dramaturg has been variously defined as "in-house critic" (Anne Cattaneo), "creative critic" (Cathy Turner and Synne Behrndt), "invisible collaborator" (Marianne Van Kerkhoven), "outside eye" (André Lepecki), "first audience" (Maaike Bleeker), and "vagrant passenger in a multi-perspective world" (Vanja Baltic). They are interlocutors between the world of the production and a public outside it, acting as an "agent in a process of communal meaning-making."[17] On the production level, which Katalin Trencsényi (building on Flemish dramaturg Van Kerkhoven) calls "micro-dramaturgy," there are two forms of dramaturgy: the new work (or development) dramaturg (Mūkonzi Mūsyoki in the diversity agent roundtable) and the production dramaturg (Anna Volkland in the PSI panel). While the new work dramaturg partners with the playwright to develop a dramatic text, the production dramaturg takes on a collaborative and hermeneutic role in the rehearsal hall to help create a performance text.[18] The production dramaturg works closely with the director to construct or analyze the text, find internal logic and inner flow within the performance, provide feedback and criticism, and serve as a consultant for background research, subject matter, internal logic, and sociopolitical implications.[19] In practice, dramaturgy engages various methods of constructive critical commentary, intervention, or engagement to *open up* possibilities for spectators in the "texture of performative proceedings."[20]

Eva Doumbia's *Le iench*, La Part du Pauvre, CDN de Normandie-Rouen, Rouen, France, 2020. Photo: Arnaud Berterau

On the level of text and production, dramaturgs are always concerned with composition and context. This is also true for their work on the institution itself.[21] The institution is not a neutral frame in which productions are presented; as Schauspielhaus's diversity agent Yuvviki Dioh says in the Performance Studies international (PSI) panel, "It's deeply embedded in society and political structures." Like the individual production, the institution is an element that the audience encounters. This encounter (itself a vision of the artistic director) is another forum for communication between audience and artwork that is also mediated by the dramaturg. Trencsényi uses the term *macro-dramaturgy* to define this overarching institutional framing, explaining, "Whereas micro-dramaturgy focuses on the dramaturgy of a piece or its dramaturgical process, macro-dramaturgy is a larger system that takes into consideration the artist, the company, the theater, its place in the community and other social and political factors."[22] These two levels intertwine and influence each other. *Institutional dramaturgy*, the term used in this issue, describes the expansion of the dramaturg's role beyond the artistic space of production into the infrastructural and institutional realm.[23] However, as theater scholar Brandon Woolf argues in his exploration of institutional transformations in Berlin's theater scene, institutional dramaturgy entails more than administrative and financial work. Instead, the ways theaters and festivals engage cultural policy "must be thought of as a performative practice of infrastructural imagining," and performances "a form of policy."[24]

The institutional dramaturg—on top of production work—takes on a curatorial role: developing and communicating a public profile as it corresponds with the institution's social, political, and artistic values, its philosophy, its programming, and how it locates itself within the community and engages with the politics of public policy.[25] As Trencsényi explains, the dramaturgy of an institution offers insight into "how it [the institution] wants to be seen and be present in the wider community . . . inseparable from the organisation's artistic policy or mission, and strongly rooted in its history and the community it serves, . . . shaped by other circumstances."[26] Veteran institutional dramaturg Matthias Lilienthal describes the institutional mise-en-scène of Castorf's Volksbühne as a "total event" aimed at openness and encounter. This institutional dramaturgy—an explicitly East German framing—was marked not only by the theater's onstage programming but also by supplementary programming: concerts, films, lectures, conferences.[27] This critical extension of the theater's frame beyond a dramatic, fictional frame and into the world beyond its walls—now common practice—

is what Christopher Balme refers to as "post-fictional" and Peter M. Boenisch as "post-representational."[28] These two framings identify a growing interest in remediating institutions to reclaim the theater's status as an "interlocutor in questions of public interest,"[29] by addressing the exclusionary structures and hierarchies—also present outside the theater—embedded within them.[30]

    Van Kerkhoven in her 1994 "State of the Union" address stated, "The theater dwells in the city and the city dwells in the world and the walls are made of skin. We cannot escape that what penetrates the pores."[31] No institution is an island. What is outside influences the inside, and the inside the outside. It is part of a city, from its origins enmeshed in its society. Cathy Turner's phenomenological concept of "porous dramaturgy" highlights the spectator's role in the cocreation of meaning. She explains a text's "intrinsic porosity" allows it to be reinterpreted in and for changing sociopolitical and historical contexts.[32] The institution is also porous. It houses artistic, social, and relational dimensions that respond to internal and external pressures and expectations.

The stage of the Pfauenbühne at Schauspielhaus Zürich, Zurich, Switzerland, 2024. Photo: T+T Photo, Juliet Haller

When the audience enters the theater or performance venue, they contend with the ghosts of artistic and social memories and accepted cultural hegemonies of an institutional present "shot through with temporal and historical logics."[33] In the porousness of micro- and macrodramaturgy—which interact and intersect—we are reminded of Boenisch's definition of institutional dramaturgy: "The institutional conditions for making as well as encountering performance, which shape symbolic, aesthetic and affective significations, practices and narratives. They relate artists and audiences, places and spaces, the present and the past—and, not the least, the global and the local."[34]

III.

Contemporary theaters—particularly in highly subsidized cultural landscapes with a responsibility to represent the taxpayers that subsidize the institutions—remain inextricably connected to their Enlightenment-era predecessors and the identities they took part in imagining. Because of colonial and imperial legacies that must still be contended with, Western Europe's cultural landscape extended beyond Europe's borders in "civilizing missions" that live on in the supposed homogeneity and (selective) universality of the colonizer's cultural norms and values.[35] Theaters in Europe and North America, as participants in the diversity agent roundtable and PSI panel note, remain white institutions, still presenting work for primarily white audiences. In their reflection on their and fellow Black migrant dramaturg Tunde Adefioye's experiences within European institutions, South African artist Kopano Maroga notes that too often the extra work of care and diversity falls onto the few BIPOC (Black, Indigenous, people of color) employees. This sentiment is echoed by London-based Latinx theater-maker Mariana Aristizábal, who has felt the responsibility to become the "representative of the oppressed" when working with different institutions.

The shifting priorities of the artistic leadership of theater and performance institutions across the globe include speaking to diversity, plurality, complexity, and conflict. They must grapple with the contradictions of white institutional attempts to bring diversity and inclusion into what is still a colonial or neocolonial frame that in many ways is at odds with innovation. For those working from the "peripheries" of former colonies like Indonesia—as Ugoran Prasad describes in his report on the Garasi Performance Institute—this means reimagining, re-forming, and revisiting both institutions and practices to reflect local traditions and decentralized contexts. Institutional leaders across the globe seek to bring the outside in, participating (or not, which also a curatorial decision) in such global movements as Occupy, #MeToo, Black Lives Matter, and protests for Palestine, and engaging with the institutional challenges raised against the often contextually specific attempts to (re)activate these institutions. Shifting institutional dramaturgy reframes the institution. It brings in outside experts like Judy Vanden Thoren to identify obstacles to inclusivity, diversity, and care; reimagines existing roles like those of the dramaturg or the artistic director; and creates new positions (diversity

officers, intimacy coordinators, cultural advocates) and departments (Indigenous theater departments; Equity, Equality, and Inclusion departments) structured around the
emergent questions of care in a sector that is constantly producing. Mairi Brascoupé,
the cultural advocate for the National Arts Center's Indigenous Theater in Ottawa,
describes how community-specific care does not necessarily follow existing institutional pathways. While in Martha Keil's article, we see how institutions—often rid-
dled with the burnout of employees working under artistic directors who burn for their
art—negotiate issues of care and innovate to present themselves as caring institutions.

The question of the future of theater and theaters of and for the future is deeply
entrenched in institutional critique and breaking from the problems of the past. Yet
as American performance artist Andrea Fraser explains, "Every time we speak of the
'institution' as other than 'us,' we disavow our role in the creation and perpetuation of
its conditions. We avoid responsibility for, or action against, the everyday complicities,
compromises, and censorship."[36] It is imperative that the innovations, transformations,
and developments described throughout this issue be regarded not as an end point but
as a starting point; or, to quote Keith Barker, these approaches must become "embedded in the practice, as opposed to something that's brought in."

Looking at the institutional dramaturgies described throughout this issue, we see
how the politics and values—elements perhaps more fluid than we recognize—of a theater are publicly and internally performed. They exemplify the intrainstitutional critique
Woolf names "dis/avowal": "the seemingly paradoxical circumstance in which artists
who receive public support make use of it to avow the administrations that govern while
simultaneously performing their transformation."[37] Practitioners using the institution
as a vehicle for institutional critique is by no means a contemporary invention. Various
avant-garde manifestos of the late nineteenth and early twentieth centuries criticized
art as an institution developed through and for bourgeois society. Likewise, numerous
examples of individual critiques have been carried into the present by a new generation
of theater artists. Bertolt Brecht's *Umfunktionierung* (functional transformation) of aesthetics remains visible in Rau's credo for engaged theater and institutional aesthetics
institutions: "It's not just about portraying the world anymore. It's about changing it. The
aim is not to depict the real, but to make the representation itself real."[38] Peter Stein's
Mitbestimmung movement marked a call, from one of the most important directors of
his generation, for collective management and power sharing, the legacy of which Noah
Lena Vercauteren identifies in renewed calls for collective leadership across the Dutch
and Flemish theater scene.[39] Alongside the near-global political swing to the right of the
mid-2010s and the steady crawl of neoliberalism's political-economic conflicts toward
the Global North's borders, a sharpening of explicit intrainstitutional critiques emerges.

Global activist movements—in which artists often play important roles—call
people to assemble in the name of ending inequality and injustice. These are mirrored
by institutions' own calls for assembly and an acknowledgment that these inequalities
are also reproduced in theaters. Given the porous nature of the relationship between

Leanna Brodie
and Jovanni Sy's
Salesman in China,
Stratford Festival,
Stratford, Ontario,
2024. Photo:
David Hou

street and institution in what Boenisch calls a "postrepresentational paradigm," theater institutions are contact and conflict zones. They are not just sites where discussion takes place; they are also active players and even a topic of discussion. Chilean artist Nelda Muray Prado, reflecting on the institutional and political landscape in which she works, highlights the complexity of the porosity between protest movements and theaters as artists become protesters and protests influence programming.

As a new generation of artistic directors attempt to break with established structures and cultural hegemonies, institutional dramaturgs must negotiate "rapidly transforming and expanding frameworks, changing audience demographics and a variety of art practices."[40] On a practical level, this means understanding the structures being worked within, against, and through, and understanding the society that surrounds the institution.[41] Marcos Davi Silva Steuernagel explores how the curators of Festival de Curitiba, one of Brazil's largest and most important theater and performance festivals, has over the past last nine years been forced to negotiate drastically different political and funding landscapes. Steuernagel describes the flexibility required to represent the diversity of Brazil's past, present, and future, contrasting Rau's construction of Festwochen as a republic that consists of Vienna but is also somehow separate from it.

It is worth noting that Europe's relationship to migration and plurality is very different from that of so-called immigrant nations of settler colonialism (e.g., the United States, Canada, Australia); from former colonies with cycles of repressive regimes (e.g., Brazil, Chile, South Africa); and from the drastically different contexts in nations like Indonesia and Japan, with their own unique relationships to colonial history as both colonized and colonizer. Postmigration offers a framework for Europe that moves beyond its existent migrant/native divide, where people two or three generations removed from migration are still seen as migrants. Instead, postmigration—both in theater and as a societal framework, as Julian Blaue notes in the PSI panel—explores how contemporary society is and always has been shaped by migration, recognizing the present's inherent plurality.[42] Yet this is not an uncontested institutional discourse. Numerous examples show the friction of this transition: Jan Goossens's rebranding of Brussels's KVS to connect with the multicultural city; Shermin Langhoff's postmigrant overhaul of Berlin's Maxim Gorki Theater; the language-based formatting of Festival d'Avignon under Tiago Rodrigues; and Benjamin von Blumberg and Nicolas Stemann's much-criticized "woke" tenure at Schauspielhaus Zürich. In this issue, Boenisch examines how a new generation of female artistic directors in Germany and Denmark are transforming city theaters into postmigrant institutions in their public profiles and the work produced. Although it is important not to limit shifts in institutional dramaturgy to Europe, across this continent the high-profile, publicly subsidized, and accepted cultural hegemony of national, royal, and city theaters has meant that institutional innovation elicits huge responses and public scandals.

IV.

Theater scandals and public backlash against new regimes of artistic directors are connected to deeply historically rooted expectations around theaters, their representational place in society, and the society they represent. In "Ghent Manifesto," Rau states, "Every institution has rules, including the theater, but they are hardly ever made public."[43] He is correct: theaters have rules that drive how they construct themselves as artistic, political, and social institutions within their respective communities. Perhaps the problem is not a lack of transparency but, rather, that they are too well known, so historically and culturally established that they seem more solid than the theater's own walls.

In her book *Understanding Institutional Diversity*, Elinor Ostrom explains, "Institutions are the prescriptions that humans use to organize all forms of repetitive and structured interactions."[44] Theater and performance are no strangers to repetition. The national and nationalistic constructions that theaters played a role in constructing were results of repetition: (re)producing plays and their accompanying bodies of knowledge, morals, and artistic traditions. Joanna Jurkiewicz and Jens Schneider explicitly state, "The understanding of culture as a stable entity interwoven with the nation-state still lies in the history and imagination of cultural institutions."[45] These institutions have over time—through the infrastructural memory and the politics of these memories, including the danger of nostalgia—become part of a habitus of "institutional rules and frameworks" while also participating in the habitus of everyday life.[46] As Balme and Tony Fisher note in *Theater Institutions in Crisis*, crisis arrives in theater when they push beyond what Jürgen Habermas names the "range of tolerance."[47] The curatorial intervention of artistic directors and institutional dramaturgs has the potential to engage with knowledge, to comment, even to intervene in the sociocultural fabric of a given society. Trencsényi explains that selecting art for a theater is "an act of criticism," which does not necessarily entail a positive reception.[48] When the range of tolerance is pushed too far, Balme and Fisher warn of a threat of collapse, a situation where "the institutional responses to challenges are so radical that they jeopardise the identity of the social system to the point that it becomes unrecognisable."[49]

Let's briefly return to the production and the dramaturg. In *Postdramatic Theatre* (1999; trans., 2006), German theorist Hans-Thies Lehmann identifies how within dramatic theater there exists a "diegetic universe," a closed fictive cosmos separate (or framed as such) from the "real" world of the audience.[50] Lehmann describes a sort of "white cube" logic of production: the creation of an insular world with its own internal logic contained in the production that the dramaturg is charged with maintaining. Balme's postfictional and Boenisch's postrepresentational paradigms identify how theater (on both the production and institutional level) break from this closed, diegetic theater world, "dispens[ing] with the cognitive apparatus required to process theatre in a fictional mode"[51] and moving institutions beyond bastions of high art to spaces that foster multiple levels of encounters.[52] Yet as sites of potential encounters, interrogations, and questioning, theater (and the arts in general) is always a political target: for exam-

Blaue & Poppy's *The Trial against Ourselves*, Kilden Teaterm Stamsund Teaterfestival, Kristiansand, Norway, 2021. Photo: Kristian Mosvold/ CourtStageTV

ple, Bolsonaro's dissolution of Brazil's Ministry of Culture on his first day in office in 2019 and the drastic cuts proposed for Berlin's world-renowned cultural sector in September 2024 as the far right reenters the political arena.[53]

The institution is not immune to a white cube paradigm that identifies the theater (which, like the white-walled gallery, is seen as hermetically sealed) as a supposedly neutral container in which timeless productions eschew certain values for specific audiences.[54] This paradigm reverberates in cultural conservative critiques of contemporary theater: the argument that theater has become too political (itself a political claim). These attacks frequently boil down to a predictable polemic against diversity: namely, that the art and status of theater (the *culture* of theater) is supposedly being cast aside, lost, or degraded in service of diversity and diversifying. The word *culture* and the concept behind it, particularly in post-Holocaust and postcolony (but not postcolonial) Europe, have since the early 1990s acted as a replacement term for *race*, highlighting the continuing connection between racial and cultural hierarchies. Echoes of this connection are heard when the work of BIPOC artists (e.g., Julia Wissert at Theater Dortmund) is described by (particularly white) critics as "simple."[55] Zoe Strimpel's "How Politics Killed Theatre" bemoans British theater "dispensing with the idea of drama, acting, or even having a stage at all" in favor of "a parade of diverse people reading angry screeds penned by activists," placing the blame squarely on "the enthusiastic take-up by arts institutions of identity politics."[56] At Rau's *Vienna Trials* (2024), retired Austrian right-wing politician Ursula Stenzel asserted that she would rather watch a "good adaptation of Büchner's *Danton's Death*" than participate, as she was doing, in "the fake trial of a communist artistic director."[57] French actor Olga Mouak described the vitriol against Rébecca Chaillon's *Carte noir (nommée désir)* at Avignon (2023) spilling out of the theater and threatening its actors' private lives. Local Swiss politicians and journalists lamented that Schauspielhaus Zürich had become "too woke, too diverse" under Stemann and von Blomberg (2019–24).[58] Matthias Lilienthal's troubled tenure at the Münchner Kammerspiele (2015–20) was plagued with critiques that he was denigrating the stage for a sociopolitical experiment.[59] The 2020 Achi Triennale's exhibition *After Freedom of Expression* was canceled after an online campaign, bomb threats, and a political campaign led by conservative politicians because of the display of two artworks deemed "anti-Japanese propaganda" in an incident reminiscent of the political and religious uproar surrounding *Caution Religion* (2003) and *Forbidden Art 2006* (2007) at Moscow's Sakharov Center.[60]

V.

Balme and Fisher identify institutional crises—both crises within institutions and those caused by institutions—as the challenges raised by structural elements that "impede, threaten, or collapse the ability of the institution to fulfil its 'proper' func-

Mariana Aristizábal's *Cansancio Tears*, MarianaMalena Theatre Company, Volcano Theatre, Ontario, Canada, 2016. Photo: Holly Revell

tions."[61] This "proper function"—like the rules of these institutions—exists as part of a shared agreement between theater and public, audience and institution. Yet this public is constantly changing, therefore the agreement is not etched in stone; it changes with its audiences. In 2014, Tom Sellar identified our entrance into a moment in which "institutions are rethinking their limitations," and theaters—whether we notice it or not—are constantly changing and adapting to the conflicts and contradictions of their audience, city, community, and politics, pushing against the limitations of a proper function.[62] Or, to quote Hansjörg Dilger and Matthais Warstat, "Institutions are never just abstract structural entities that regulate and orient societies independently of human intervention. Rather, they consist of the actions and agreements of numerous individuals, who rather than always taking these institutions for granted can reflect on how they came into being historically and choose to redefine their natures and relations."[63] As a critical lens, institutional dramaturgy offers a path to interrogate systemic modifications and better understand the theater's changing role and cultural relevance.[64] For this critical theory, identifying change within established practices is key. In discussions of these stratified structures, the term *canonization* frequently appears in relation to stagnation, but these institutions also possess the power to canonize and normalize texts, productions, artists, and even institutional practices.[65]

This issue takes an expansive glance at the conversations, transformations, realities, and practices on, in, and around institutional dramaturgy on local and global stages. Engagement with the critiques inherently present in scholarly and practice-based discussions of institutional dramaturgy entails an awareness that theaters reproduce violent social, colonial, political, and cultural structures. It also involves grappling with the means and relations of production to disrupt and change these structures.[66] It means recognizing that because of the porosity of institutions and dramaturgies, that agents of change—like agents of stagnation—come from both inside and outside the theater. Amid the shifting tides of a mobile, conflictual, plural, and polarized present that theater institutions must contend with, perhaps the most important point is Andrea Fraser's poignant reflection in her 2005 article "From the Critique of Institutions to an Institution of Critique" on intrainstitutional critique, which we should also

Moved by the Motion's *Carmen*, Schauspielhaus Zürich, Zurich, Switzerland, 2023. Photo: Ines Manai

extend to what scholarship asks of theater and scholarship itself: "It's not a question of being against the institution: We are the institution. It's a question of what kind of institution we are, what kind of values we institutionalize, what forms of practice we reward, and what kinds of rewards we aspire to."[67]

Notes

1. Ute Büsing, "Ende der Ära Castorf an der Berliner Volksbühne," *DW*, July 1, 2017, https://www.dw.com/de/berserker-provokateur-theaterrevoluzzer-volksb%C3%BChnen -chef-frank-castorf-geht/a-39454841.

2. Eva Marburg, "Volksbühne sucht neue Leitung: Die Stellenausschreibung spricht Bände," *Der Freitag*, September 17, 2024, https://www.freitag.de/autoren/eva-marburg /volksbuehne-in-berlin-sucht-intendanz-stellenausschreibung-spricht-baende.

3. Rüdiger Schaper, "Volksbühne Tim Renner will am 30. April Castorf-Nachfolger vorstellen," *Tagesspiegel*, April 22, 2015, https://www.tagesspiegel.de/kultur/tim-renner -will-am-30-april-castorf-nachfolger-vorstellen-6889318.html; "Intendant mit Tanz und Hangar," *Nachkritik*, April 22–23, 2015, https://nachtkritik.de/meldungen2/meldungen-k /chris-dercon-soll-intendant-der-volksbuehne-werden.

4. Sven Lütticken, "Art as Immoral Institution," *Texte zur Kunst*, October 3, 2017, https:// www.textezurkunst.de/en/articles/sven-lutticken-volksbuhne-occupation/.

5. Peter M. Boenisch, "Struggles of Singularised Communities in German Theatre," in *Theatre Institutions in Crisis: European Perspectives*, ed. Christopher Balme and Tony Fisher (London: Routledge, 2021), 38; Wolfgang Höbel, "Gescheitert am borniertem Berlin," *Spiegel Kultur*, April 13, 2018, https://www.spiegel.de/kultur/gesellschaft/chris -dercon-verlaesst-volksbuehne-scheinsieg-der-theater-verwahrer-a-1202799.html; Monisha Caroline Martins, "The Curtain Falls on the Occupation of Berlin's Historic Volksbühne," *OpenDemocracy*, October 5, 2017, https://www.opendemocracy.net/en/can -europe-make-it-curtain-falls-on-occupation-of-berlin-s-historic-volksb-/; Robert Klages, "Zukunft der Volksbühne," *Tagesspiegel*, June 17, 2019, https://www.tagesspiegel .de/kultur/der-traum-vom-kollektiven-theater-5021698.html; Colette M. Schmidt, "Intendant René Pollesch startet auf der Volksbühne," *Der Standard*, September 17, 2021, https://www.derstandard.de/story/2000129743608/intendant-rene-pollesch-startet-auf -der-volksbuehne-neuer-stoff-am.

6. "Der Senat schrietet ein," *taz*, March 14, 2021, https://taz.de/Sexistische-Uebergriffe -an-der-Volksbuehne/!5757843/; Kate Connolly, "Berlin Volksbühne Theatre Director Resigns over Harassment Claims," *Guardian*, March 16, 2021, https://www.theguardian .com/world/2021/mar/16/berlin-volksbuhne-theatre-director-resigns-over-harassment -claims; Rüdiger Schaper, "Beschwerden von zehn Frauen," *Tagesspiegel*, March 13, 2021, https://www.tagesspiegel.de/kultur/metoo-vorwurfe-gegen-intendanten-der-berliner -volksbuhne-5392393.html.

7. Sandra Sarala, "The Return of the Volksbühne," *Berliner*, December 17, 2021, https:// www.the-berliner.com/stage/the-return-of-the-volksbuhne/; Rüdiger Schaper, "Trauerspiel in Endlosschleife," *Tagesspiegel*, June 4, 2022, https://www.tagesspiegel.de /kultur/rene-pollesch-und-die-volksbuhne-grotte-in-weimar-499659.html; Janis

El-Bira and Esther Slevogt, "Im Bann der Erinnyen," *Nachtkritik*, July 8, 2022, https://nachtkritik.de/recherche-debatte/debatte-um-die-volksbuehne.

8. Rüdiger Schaper, "Befreiungsschlag an der Volksbühne," *Tagesspiegel*, October 4, 2024, https://www.tagesspiegel.de/kultur/befreiungsschlag-an-der-volksbuhne-vegard-vinge -und-ida-muller-ubernehmen-die-leitung-12483290.html; Ulrich Seidler, "Verheerender Kulturhaushalt: Vinge und Müller verzichten auf Interimsintendanz der Volksbühne," *Berliner Zeitung*, December 2, 2024, https://www.berliner-zeitung.de/kultur-vergnuegen /theater/volksbuehne-vinge-und-mueller-verzichten-wegen-verheerendem-kulturhaushalt -auf-interimsintendanz-li.2277681; Janis El-Bira, "Eventbude 2.0?," *Nachtkritik*, February 7, 2025, https://www.nachtkritik.de/recherche-debatte/kommentar-matthias-lilienthal -uebernimmt-die-berliner-volksbuehne.

9. Tanja Bogusz, "Eine Bühne des Volks? Oder des Erfolgs im Kapitalismus? Zur Debatte über die Volksbühne," *Berliner Gazette*, June 1, 2015, https://berlinergazette.de /de/volk-oder-kapitalismus/.

10. Cathy Turner and Synne Behrndt, *Dramaturgy and Performance*, rev. ed. (London: Palgrave, 2016), 102.

11. Turner and Behrndt, *Dramaturgy and Performance*, 25.

12. Erika Fischer-Lichte, Christel Weiler, and Torsten Jost, "Dramaturgies of Interweaving: Engaging Audiences in an Entangled World," in *Dramaturgies of Interweaving: Engaging Audiences in an Entangled World* (London: Routledge, 2021), 1; Katalin Trencsényi, *Dramaturgy in the Making: A User's Guide for Theatre Practitioners* (London: Bloomsbury, 2015), 5–7.

13. Trencsényi, *Dramaturgy in the Making*, 5–6, 13; Loren Kruger, *The National Stage: Theatre and Cultural Legitimation in England, France, and America* (Chicago: University of Chicago Press, 1992), 6–8.

14. Vanja Baltic, "The Dramaturg's Gaze: About the Role of the Dramaturg in Contemporary Theatre and Dance Practice," *Antropologia e Teatro* 9 (2018): 124.

15. Trencsényi, *Dramaturgy in the Making*, 14.

16. Eda Čufer, "Petnajst lepih tez o dramaturgiji," *Maska*, nos. 1–2 (2001): 23.

17. Adrian Heathfield, "Dramaturgy without a Dramaturg," *Theatre Times*, August 15, 2016, https://thetheatretimes.com/dramaturgy-without-a-dramaturg/.

18. Ann-Christine Simke, "Institutional Dramaturgy at the Deutsches Theater Berlin," in *Dramaturgies of War: Institutional Dramaturgy, Politics, and Conflict in Twentieth-Century Germany*, ed. Anselm Heinrich and Ann-Christine Simke (London: Palgrave, 2024), 14.

19. Trencsényi, *Dramaturgy in the Making*, 124–25; Katalin Trencsényi and Bernadette Cochrane, "Foreword. New Dramaturgy: A Post-mimetic, Intercultural, Process-Conscious Paradigm," in *New Dramaturgy: International Perspectives on Theory and Practice* (London: Bloomsbury, 2014), xxi; Turner and Behrndt, *Dramaturgy and Performance*, 21.

20. Fischer-Lichte, Weiler, and Jost, "Dramaturgies of Interweaving," 1.

21. Turner and Behrndt, *Dramaturgy and Performance*, 124.

22. Trencsényi, *Dramaturgy in the Making*, 259.

23. Konstantina Georgelou, Efrosini Protopapa, and Danae Theodoridou, *The Practice of Dramaturgy: Working on Actions in Performance* (Amsterdam: Valiz, 2017), 3.

24. Brandon Woolf, *Institutional Theatrics: Performing Arts Policy in Post-Wall Berlin* (Evanston, IL: Northwestern University Press, 2021), 8.

25. Trencsényi, *Dramaturgy in the Making*, 35; Simke, "Institutional Dramaturgy," 14.

26. Trencsényi, *Dramaturgy in the Making*, 32.

27. Lilienthal quoted in Woolf, *Institutional Theatrics*, 76–77.

28. Christopher Balme, "Postfictional Theatre, Institutional Aesthetics, and the German Theatrical Public Sphere," *TDR* 67, no. 2 (2023): 16–17.

29. Balme, "Postfictional Theatre," 29.

30. Peter Boenisch, "Theatre Curation and Institutional Dramaturgy: Post-Representation Transformations in Flemish Theatre," *Peripeti* 19, no. 35 (2022), 79.

31. Marianne Van Kerkhoven quoted in Christel Stalpaert, "A Dramaturgy of the Body," *Performance Research* 14, no. 3 (2009): 124.

32. Cathy Turner, "Porous Dramaturgy and the Pedestrian," in *New Dramaturgy: International Perspectives on Theory and Practice*, ed. Katalin Trencsényi and Bernadette Cochrane (London: Bloomsbury, 2014), 205.

33. Christopher Balme and Tony Fisher, "Introduction," in *Theatre Institutions in Crisis: European Perspectives*, ed. Balme and Fisher (London: Routledge, 2021), 25.

34. Peter M. Boenisch, "Encountering a 'Theater of (Inter-)Singularity': Transformations and Rejections of Shifting Institutional Dramaturgies in Contemporary German Theater," in *Dramaturgies of Interweaving* (London: Routledge, 2022), 158.

35. Kira Kosnick, "New Year's Eve, Sexual Violence and Moral Panics: Ruptures and Continuities in Germany's Integration Regime," in *Refugees Welcome? Difference and Diversity in a Changing Germany*, ed. Jan-Jonathan Bock and Sharon Macdonald (New York: Berghahn Books, 2019), 175.

36. Andrea Fraser, "From the Critique of Institutions to an Institution of Critique," *Artforum* 44, no. 1 (2005), https://www.artforum.com/features/from-the-critique-of -institutions-to-an-institution-of-critique-172201/.

37. Brandon Woolf, *Institutional Theatrics: Performing Arts Policy in Post-Wall Berlin* (Evanston, IL: Northwestern University Press, 2021), 11.

38. Marvin Carlson, *Theatre Is More Beautiful than War: German Stage Directing in the Late Twentieth Century* (Iowa City: University of Iowa Press, 2009), 50; Milo Rau, "The Ghent Manifesto," *Theater* 52, no. 2 (2021): 23.

39. Paul Haacke, "The Brechtian Exception: From Weimar to the Cold War," *Diacritics* 40, no. 3 (2012): 59.

40. Trencsényi, *Dramaturgy in the Making*, 31.

41. Bertie Ferdman, "From Content to Context: The Emergence of the Performance Curator," in *Curating Live Arts: Critical Perspectives, Essays, and Conversations on Theory and Practice*, ed. Dena Davida, Marc Pronovost, Véronique Hudon, and Jane Gabriels (New York: Berghahn Books, 2018), 25.

42. Naika Foroutan, "The Post-migrant Paradigm," in *Refugees Welcome? Difference and Diversity in a Changing Germany*, ed. Jan-Jonathan Bock and Sharon MacDonald (New York: Berghahn Books, 2019), 148, 153; Hansjörg Dilger and Matthias Warstat, "Affective Diversity: Conceptualizing Institutional Change in Postmigrant Societies," in *Affect, Power, and Institutions*, ed. Millicent Churcher, Sandra Calkins, Jandra Böttger, and Jan Slaby (London: Routledge, 2022), 231.

43. Rau, "Ghent Manifesto," 21.

44. Elinor Ostrom, *Understanding Institutional Diversity* (Princeton, NJ: Princeton University Press, 2006), 3.

45. Joanna Jurkiewicz and Jens Schneider, "On Continuities: Migration and Institutional (Non-)Change," in *Cultural Change in Post-migrant Societies: Re-imagining Communities through Arts and Cultural Activities*, ed. Wiebke Sievers (Cham, Switzerland: Springer, 2023), 80.

46. Christopher Balme, "Theatrical Institutions in Motion: Developing Theatre in the Postcolonial Era," *Journal of Dramatic Theory and Criticism* 31, no. 2 (2017): 129–30; Woolf, *Institutional Theatrics*, 121.

47. Habermas, quoted in Balme and Fisher, "Introduction," 23.

48. Trencsényi, *Dramaturgy in the Making*, 32.

49. Balme and Fisher, "Introduction," 23–24.

50. Hans-Thies Lehmann, *Postdramatic Theatre*, trans. Karen Jürs-Munby (London: Routledge, 2006), 99–100.

51. Balme, "Postfictional Theatre," 18–19.

52. Boenisch, "Theatre Curation," 73.

53. "Berlin: Bühnenverein protestiert gegen drastische Sparauflagen," *Nachkritiken*, September 26, 2024, https://nachtkritik.de/meldungen/berlin-buehnenverein-protestiert -gegen-drastische-sparauflagen.

54. See Brian O'Doherty, *Inside the White Cube: The Ideology of the Gallery Space* (Santa Monica, CA: Lapis Press, 1986).

55. Kosnick, "New Year's Eve," 175.

56. Zoe Strimpel, "How Politics Killed Theatre," *Spectator*, October 15, 2022, https:// www.spectator.co.uk/article/how-politics-killed-theatre/.

57. Ursula Stenzel, "Die Wiener Prozesse / 2. Prozess / Anschläge auf die Demokratie," Wiener Festwochen, live-streamed on June 9, 2024, YouTube, 2:07:41, https://www .youtube.com/watch?v=sJe4cPN-hek.

58. Andreas Klaeui, "Publikumsgipfel in Zürich," *SRF*, January 19, 2023, https://www .srf.ch/kultur/buehne/publikumsgipfel-in-zuerich-zu-woke-zu-divers-was-will-das -publikum-vom-schauspielhaus.

59. Christine Dössel, "Kammerspiele? Jammerspiele!," *Süddeutsche Zeitung*, November 11, 2016, https://www.sueddeutsche.de/kultur/theaterkrise-in-muenchen-kammerspiele -jammerspiele-1.3243228.

60. Tadasu Takahashi, "Freedom of Expression and the 2019 Aichi Triennale," *Tokyo Review*, May 8, 2020, https://www.tokyoreview.net/2020/05/aichi-triennale-2019 -freedom-expression/.

61. Balme and Fisher, "Introduction," 22.

62. Tom Sellar, "The Curatorial Turn," *Theater* 44, no. 2 (2014): 22.

63. Dilger and Warstat, "Affective Diversity," 241.

64. Peter M. Boenisch, "Theatre Curation and Institutional Dramaturgy: Post-representational Transformations in Flemish Theatre," *Peripeti* 19, no. 35 (2022): 72; Woolf, *Institutional Theatrics*, 11.

65. Trencsényi, *Dramaturgy in the Making*, 32.

66. Woolf, *Institutional Theatrics*, 83.

67. Fraser, "From the Critique."

Julia Wissert's
*2170—Was wird die
Stadt gewesen sein, in
der wir leben werden?*
(*2170—What Will
the City Have Been in
Which We Will Have
Lived?*), Schauspiel
Dortmund,
Dortmund, Germany,
2020. Photo: Birgit
Hupfeld

PETER M. BOENISCH

INSTITUTIONAL DRAMATURGIES IN GERMAN AND DANISH THEATER

Negotiating Cultural Plurality and Systemic Hierarchies

Theaters across Europe face what art critic Nora Sternfeld describes as their "post-representational" transformation: In contrast to the earlier "postdramatic" turn, this shift does not concern the aesthetic form but points towards considerable shifts in the infrastructural and institutional frameworks of producing theatre. Drawing on the postmodern critique of representation as a mechanism that constitutes cultural "normalities," standards, and therefore also exclusions, Sternfeld analyses contests over representational strategies where theaters (as well as museums and other cultural institutions) no longer unproblematically represent national grandeur, civic *Bildung*, and (white) middle-class cultural capital.[1] They are confronted with, among other developments, shifting audience demographics, changing cultural habits resulting not least from the pervasiveness of social and digital media, and turbulences in the political public sphere with its clashes between power-critical decolonization and antidemocratic radicalization. Our research project at Aarhus University's Department of Dramaturgy, Reconfiguring Dramaturgy for a Global Culture: Changing Practices in Twenty-First Century European Theater, observed how theaters in Germany, Belgium, Portugal, Sweden, and Denmark respond to this challenge by developing new institutional politics of extended, plural representation. In this article I introduce two examples: Schauspiel Dortmund and the Betty Nansen Teatret. Schauspiel Dortmund is a typical German city theater located in the Ruhr area. It has been led since 2020 by Julia Wissert, the first Black German (and at her appointment also youngest) artistic director in the German public theater system, who strives for making city theater for the entire city. The Betty Nansen Teatret in Frederiksberg, within the greater Copenhagen area, dates back to a nineteenth-century Danish boulevard theater. Since 2018, its leadership duo of Elisa Kragerup and Eva Præstiin has pioneered nonhierarchical production modes. Applying the lens of institutional dramaturgy allows us to capture the shifts in the professional role and required competencies of theater dramaturgs, as

Theater 55:2 DOI 10.1215/01610775-11683481

their work more and more extends beyond the classical focus on script and production development not only toward audience development but even more so toward post-representational (re)developments of the theater institution itself. At the same time, dramaturgy—as the competence to articulate and represent dramatic conflicts in both fictional and real worlds—becomes a potent tool for navigating the sometimes dramatic conflicts caused by shifting (and hence often competing) institutional values, which frame and impact on creative decisions and the conditions for artistic production.

GERMAN THEATER: ART FOR THE CULTURED "CORE" OR A POLYPHONY FOR THE ENTIRE CITY?

Typically for Germany's state-funded theater landscape, Schauspiel (drama) Dortmund is one of six departments within the larger "Theater Dortmund" institutional entity, sharing administrative and technical infrastructure; the other departments are the opera, ballet, philharmonic orchestra, the children's and youth theater, and the academy for digital theater. The Schauspiel currently employs twelve ensemble actors and is home to the associated mixed-ability company I Can Be Your Translator as well as a community ensemble of around one hundred local citizens. In her application pitch for the position, artistic director Julia Wissert (b. 1984) had focused on her intention to create city theater that represents the *entire* city. She proposed the notion of "polyphony" as core metaphor for her attempts to break through the usual uniform dominance of white, well-educated middle-class audiences and theater-makers.[2] This seems particularly apt for Dortmund, a city of some 580,000 inhabitants with a long history of work migration and transcontinental trade links that date back to the thirteenth century, when it was a key driver in the mercantilist trade network of the Hanseatic League; it then, with its neighboring cities in the Ruhr Valley, became a center of industrialization, coal mining, and heavy industry that defined its identity until the deindustrialization of the late twentieth century. Wissert dedicated a position within the dramaturgy department to appoint a "city dramaturg," tasked with establishing links to art and community spaces that so far had had little connection with the theater, and with sourcing themes and concerns in the wider city environment that may inspire productions.

Wissert's intent to turn the theater into "a space that is being curated by the city" became evident in her opening production in autumn 2020, *2170—What Will the City Have Been Like, in Which We Are Going to Live?*[3] Due to pandemic restrictions at the time, it was staged as walking *parcour* through Dortmund's inner city. Small audience groups passed places of often-disavowed past and present histories, such as the site of the Jewish synagogue destroyed in 1938 (now the location of the opera house), a memorial for victims of the National Socialist Underground neo-Nazi murders of the 2000s, notorious postwar high-rise buildings, and the main train station, whose railway lines very symbolically cut the multicultural and less prosperous northern district off from

Exterior facade of Schauspiel Dortmund, Dortmund, Germany. Photo: Birgit Hupfeld

the rest of the city. At these sites, the audience encountered performances of short texts commissioned from contemporary playwrights that were framed by the imaginary scenario of looking back at the present and coming decades from a distant perspective 150 years away, in 2170. Once able to return to the Schauspiel's two (main and studio) stages, productions such as *Under Ground*, created by Amsterdam-based performance artist Sanja Mitrović in 2023, further evidenced the local focus. This piece combined a narrative around the city's last coal mine (closed in 2018) with a dystopian future, where as a result of the climate catastrophe human life retreats into the old underground tunnels. Exemplifying the likewise "polyphonic" take on the canonical repertoire, *Between Two Tempests*, directed in 2021 by a former collaborator of Christoph Schlingensief, Poutiaire Lionel Somé from Burkina Faso, responded to both Shakespeare and Aimé Césaire's 1969 Négritude retelling from a third perspective, with Dortmund-based Black storyteller Bernice Lysania Ekoula Akouala as central figure of Sycorax, who meets (among others) a Miranda character with clear references to young climate activists. A further strand in the theater's repertoire, and today the most successful one, is the production of plays and adaptations of novels by contemporary German writers of diverse backgrounds, such as Necati Öziri, Nora Abdel-Maksoud, Hengameh Yaghoobifarah, and Sharon Dodua Otoo. The focus on plurality equally led to a series of now-annual festivals dedicated to feminism, queer culture, and, with "Dortmund Goes Black," to the city's people of color. They have become platforms for community debates and meetings not just about art and theater but also about life and living in present-day Dortmund, while also connecting with local artists whose work does not fit the standard genres usually presented at dramatic theaters, such as storytelling.

Working outside a major metropolitan center such as Berlin, and with more limited resources, Schauspiel Dortmund thus experiments with implementing "postrepresentational" theater into its daily work routine. Emphasizing social plurality and thereby extending prior agendas in recent German theater, such as the postmigrant work defined by Berlin's Maxim Gorki Theater, Wissert and her team turned the Schauspiel both externally and internally, according to Mary Louise Pratt's much-cited terminology, from an affirmative cultural "comfort zone" into a rather turbulent "contact zone." Not just onstage but also in rehearsal rooms and technical workshops, a range of narratives, meanings, histories, and abilities meet and often clash in contests over values, priorities, norms, and alternatives. As dramaturg Viktoria Göke notes, dramaturgs act as crucial links of such polyphonic theater work, not least with the standardized organizational working practices in the technical departments. Instead of being the traditional intellectual knowledge banks, they are in demand due to their skills as mediators,

Poutiaire Lionel Somé's *Zwischen zwei Stürmen* (*Between Two Tempests*), Schauspiel Dortmund, Dortmund, Germany, 2021. Photo: Birgit Hupfeld

negotiators, and facilitators.[4] They get support from a diversity manager, Ella Steinmann, whom the Schauspiel now employs. Her main task is not the diversification of audiences but the management of organizational practices within the institution, for instance when a white dramaturg finds that she is the only non–person of color in the rehearsal room during the theater's 2023 production of *Eternity, the End and Everything That Never Began*, created by US American performance duo Ta-Nia. Or when a director with Down syndrome, Linda Fisahn, stages Shakespeare's *Romeo and Juliet* for and with people with diverse abilities.

Julia Wissert observes that now longtime employees in backstage departments have also begun to embrace her attempts to rethink systemic organizational practices.[5] Meanwhile, dramaturg Viktoria Göke tries to communicate new criteria for promoting the postrepresentational city theater art among audiences used to "their" Shakespeares and Ibsens. She engages audience members in courses at the local community college, where they can follow production processes such as Fisahn's encounter with *Romeo and Juliet*, or the work on Ibsen's *Enemy of the People* (2024) by director Babett Grube and the German-Afro-American author Julienne De Muirier. During rehearsals, the play's political focus flipped into a resistance against the privileged political machinations of Ibsen's medic, mayor, journalists, and local politicians, to instead give voice to the bath's workers as they deal with the plot's viral outbreak. Such new and at times still imperfect perspectives, especially on repertoire classics, emerge not from usual *Regietheater* deconstruction but from a play's confrontation with greater range of the artists and makers' life experiences. The dramaturgs' mediation of these encounters also invites, as Göke notes, the rethinking of the audiences' evaluation criteria to make sense of these productions in different ways, which she observes many then also communicate to other spectators.

Still others, predictably, lament their thwarted expectations, or even violently resist what they perceive as the takeover of "their" theater by a "woke" Black theater leader. Again the *Süddeutsche Zeitung*, the German national newspaper instrumental in terminating the artistic directorships of Matthias Lilienthal at Münchner Kammerspiele and of other German theater-makers seeking systemic transformations, acts as a mouthpiece of such pseudoliberal rejection. Claiming it was impossible to critique the Black artistic director without being called out as racist, the paper sought, through a one-year undercover investigation, to demolish Wissert's reputation with claims of financial mismanagement and misuse of power in office, which were eventually rebutted by the theater management, union representatives, and the city's mayor of culture alike, but nevertheless served as ammunition for a reactionary public to demand Wissert's dismissal. Elsewhere, critic Till Briegleb, in the leading journal of the German theater establishment, *Theater heute*, raised his voice against the work of "socially and politically motivated artistic directors," explicitly naming Wissert and other theater leaders, predominantly female. He instead considers it the "civic duty of theater spectators" to cultivate their "basic educated curiosity that is needed in order not to feel out of place in the theater":

> The core audiences of German city theaters demand from the productions a certain intellectual level. . . . Where the matured quality standards of the European theater are constantly simplified in order not to exclude anyone, the institution loses its soul—and its audience. This is why theaters will never represent the "entire" society . . . but only ever those who on a path toward their somewhat civilized existence want to see themselves reflected in stage works.[6]

While constant allegations of making things complicated, let alone ad hominem attacks, have taken their toll on Wissert, she is relentlessly determined to stick to the ambitious transformation of her theater, to the point where these changes will leave a legacy beyond her own tenure as artistic director.[7] For Wissert, it is evident that theaters must move beyond "perpetuating an idea of a German society that never existed: that is white, male, Christian, cis, and just unambiguously normal. . . . Today the world we knew is getting more complex through emancipatory movements, and we can either embrace them or become obsolete."[8] The city theater, for her, is the very place to come together, to imagine and thereby negotiate and find answers to these societal transformations: "to get comfortable with the uncomfortable."[9]

DANISH THEATER: DEVELOPING ARTISTIC ALLIANCES IN AESTHETIC COMMUNITIES

The urge to challenge an organizational environment used to standardized production modes and conventional stage languages is also evident in developments in Danish theater, whose far lighter institutional infrastructure (compared with the organizational complexity of German theater), combined with less direct influence from elected party politicians and greater powers afforded to boards of directors, has enabled several recent appointments to artistic leadership positions. In those new artistic leaders, aesthetic originality (often expressly inspired by German theater) and a vision for transformative production modes go hand in hand. Just before the COVID hiatus, Sargun Oshana (b. 1984) became Denmark's first artistic director with a migrant background, at Teater Grob, which he relaunched as Blaagaard Teater, renamed after the street outside in the culturally diverse Copenhagen district of Nørrebro, whose impulses Oshana infuses into the "new work" the theater is dedicated to. In the same year, Liv Helm (b. 1985) took over the intimate Husets Teater, founded in 1975 to stage classical and new European drama, a tradition she continues with dedicated focus on feminist values of care and sustainability. And just outside Copenhagen, in Allerød in North Zealand, the twenty-seven-year-old Anna Malzer became Denmark's youngest artistic director, at Mungo Park, an alternative theater dating from the 1970s. She brought in a younger, more diverse ensemble to create largely devised works on current topics, with which she intends to engage nontraditional spectators in the less privileged Copenhagen periphery by also touring productions to nontheater spaces.

Looking back at interviews with the new leaders, it is notable that all three do not simply foreground individual aesthetics but emphasize their intentions to work beyond the boundaries of artistic disciplines and established genres, and to transform the ways of producing theater. They all refer to the pioneering work of Elisa Kragerup and Eva Præstiin, since 2018 artistic director and theater producer, respectively, of Frederiksberg's Betty Nansen Teatret. Both had previously been with the Red Room, a collective of performers, directors, scenographers, dramaturgs, and lighting designers, who had been given free rein, over five seasons, to collectively run a small stage at the Danish Royal Theater, before the experiment was closed in 2016 with the advent of a new artistic director. Kragerup and Præstiin were subsequently appointed to the Betty Nansen, one of five theaters that form the self-owned, state-supported Copenhagen Theatre Cooperation in the greater region around Denmark's capital. Here they sought to introduce the Red Room's alternative, cocreative approaches into the organizational structure of a larger institution with three stages (the five-hundred-seat main house, the

Anna Balslev's *Stoldhed og fordom* (*Pride and Prejudice*), Betty Nansen Teatret, Copenhagen, Denmark, 2024. Photo: Camilla Winther

two-hundred-seventy-seat Edison annex, and the hundred-seat Silo studio). Today their theater has, in addition to the directors, sixteen permanent employees, all in the administrative and technical backstage, since Kragerup and Præstiin shifted entirely toward project-based production with a network of freelance artists. Concentrating on production structures, their interventions were less encompassing than Wissert's; above all, they did not interfere with the theater's established artistic identity, seeking to still offer the expected "contemporary drama and classics with a twist."[10]

This new twist results from their collective approach based on "artistic alliances," which they eventually branded "Betty Udvikler" (Betty Develops). They dropped the standard five-week rehearsal periods and tried to move away from the usual dominance of a core creative team (of director, playwright, scenographer) in a production process designed to serve the concept they had brought in. Instead, the "Udvikler" principle is based on bringing creative teams together for a series of workshops that may span between some months and a couple of years before the eventual premiere. Here the teams together define themes and gradually develop ideas, some of which might be dropped or altered if they turn out not to work. Through these workshops emerge what Præstiin calls "beta versions" of future productions.[11] The starting point for any production at Betty Nansen Teatret is now always such an arranged meeting of artists rather than the choice of a specific play or text to be produced. The definition of a research question as common reference point, as well as agreeing rules for the collaborative work, have become core coordinates of the "Udvikler" approach.

Drawing from philosophical concepts—Kragerup and Præstiin refer in particular to Donna Haraway's principle of "making-with" and Jacques Rancière's "aesthetic communities"—collectivity is here considered not as flat equality but as "co-creation between a community of strong and often opposing individuals."[12] The director's main role becomes that of facilitator, still retaining the final word on artistic decisions, which can still be debated by the plenum of collaborators. As Præstiin notes, this mode of collective work requires each participant's readiness to step back and be led, while also being sensitive about when it is necessary to take the initiative.[13] Regarding their own, usually pivotal role as theater leaders—where Wissert at Dortmund experiences the dilemma of feeling like "the queen introducing democracy"[14]—Præstiin and Kragerup installed an artistic advisory board, whose six members come from various theater and related professions, including an academic and a journalist. This council has replaced the dramaturgy department; it proposes the teams of creative talents who are then invited for an initial workshop to explore a prospective collaboration. Based on this production mode, Betty Nansen Teatret creates six to eight productions each season, which run en suite. The 2023–24 program included Simon Stephens's *Maria*, Marlowe's *Edward II*, and adaptions of Jane Austen's *Pride and Prejudice* and Lewis Carroll's *Alice's Adventures in Wonderland*. The latter, for example, emerged from a workshop meeting of a director, a choreographer, and performers who toyed with nonhuman physicalities. As in Schauspiel Dortmund's programming, a preponderance of adaptations in the theater's programming is evident.

Amanda Ginman's *ALICE*, Betty Nansen Teatret, Copenhagen, Denmark, 2024. Photo: Camilla Winther

A (meanwhile renewed) grant from the philanthropic Bikuben Foundation sustains the employment of a dedicated project leader to coordinate, document, and publish the activities of "Betty Udvikler." Similar to Wissert's ambition, the theater also aspires to introduce structural transformation that does not remain tied to the current leadership but instead contributes to a wider organizational shift. The resulting publications, mostly disseminated online (some also in English translation), such as the resource guide *Eight Paths to Collective Co-Creation*, books on giving feedback in production processes and on collective leadership, and a documentary film about the "Udvikler principle," have become essential resources also for Danish theater education, particularly outside conservatoire training, including production classes at our dramaturgy department. Transitioning into a second five-year tenure at the helm of Betty Nansen Teatret, Kragerup and Præstiin summed up the transformations of their first five years in a concise manifesto: it states three core values, describing the work at Betty Nansen Teatret as polyphonic, physical, and feminist, where the latter term is explained not only in relation to gender but also as "diversity, equality, and care."[15]

Over the years, the theater has also launched attempts to integrate their production values into its engagement with audiences. The theater arranges events and theme nights aligned with the productions (frequently participatory, often inviting audiences to dress up accordingly), and they commission what they call "sister works" that complement current stage productions in other media, on film, in social media, as music compositions or documentaries, and in other genres, taking prompts from the productions' themes or characters. The venue itself, meanwhile, presents itself as an open community hub, hosting concerts and other events under the name "Confetti Betty." Above all, the public presentation of the theater as a persona, referring to itself consistently as "Betty," and an according engagement work via social media have led to an extensive reach, and not least a new local hype around the theater's namesake Betty Nansen (1873–1943), the Danish contemporary of great actresses such as Sarah Bernhardt and Eleonora Duse. Nansen was the theater's director from 1917 until her death, and in 2022 she was honored with a bronze statue in the city, unveiled by then Danish queen Margarete II. The theater managed to make more than twenty-eight thousand members sign up for its free scheme "Our Betty," giving access to early booking, reduced prices and special events, demonstrating a successful change of mind from old exclusive subscriber approaches toward a contemporary "follower" tribe, supported by a vibe of constant events—inevitably a communicative foundation to support the systemic transformation.

Institutional Dramaturgy: Staying with Postrepresentational Troubles

Compared to the wide publicity about Julia Wissert's work, the changes at Betty Nansen Teatret were never as hotly debated. Conflicts that resulted from the shifting work approach remained largely confined to the workshop spaces; press publications focus nearly exclusively on the productions and artistic work. As Eva Præstiin notes, their innovative production modes were less noticed by audiences, whose principal focus remain the performances onstage.[16] Hence, the theater never found itself engulfed, like Schauspiel Dortmund, within a far wider societal culture clash—but it also did not make as radical attempts to rethink access, participation, and ownership of a privileged cultural institution, at all levels at once. When Danish people-of-color actors and artists—most of whom also very active on and behind the Danish stage—in 2023 confronted the structural racism in the country's film industry with the initiative *A*

Bigger Picture,[17] their diagnoses equally put the finger on blind spots in Danish theater, which has yet to see its "postmigrant moment" that transformed systemic theater structures in Germany and numerous other European countries over the past decade. The development of new, less hierarchical cocreative production modes practiced and promoted by the Betty Nansen Teatret, however, has laid the already noted important ground that then inspired a younger generation to take further steps: the work of Sargun Oshana, Anna Malzer, and Liv Helm has been mentioned. On the back of a now widely embraced discourse of more sustainable working practices, which was principally driven by the work at the Betty Nansen Teatret, they also began to raise debates about structurally perpetuated gender, cultural, and class privileges within the Danish theater system. Resonating with the spirit of recent #MeToo and Black Lives Matter movements also in Scandinavia, their innovations then encouraged further demands—for instance, demands for more plurality among students at the Danish National Academy of Performing Arts.

Such a slower, step-by-step approach to gradually extending systemic transformation contrasts with the local ad hoc rupture that Schauspiel Dortmund has implemented, causing conflicts even within their own Theater Dortmund infrastructure. These contrasting paths taken by the two theaters reflect the differing contexts of the small, more dynamic (yet in other respects far more conservative) Danish theater system and the large, heavy institutional structures of German theater production (which still allowed the relative quick adoption of postmigrant participation as new norm, resulting not least in Wissert's appointment). Similar "slow" initiatives in German theater—for instance, by Anna Bergmann, former director at Badisches Staatstheater Karlsruhe, who only worked with female directors and equally aimed for the introduction of more sustainable production modes—indeed remained locally confined, rarely leaving a legacy beyond the respective artistic leader's tenure.[18]

Amanda Ginman's *ALICE*. Photo: Camilla Winther

What unites the two theaters discussed here are their sustained efforts to extend what had been previously tested as cocreative or polyphonic approaches within contexts of singular productions to the deep systemic fabric of large organizational structures, and to turn these principles into normalized institutional working practices.

Julienne De Muirier's *Ein Volksfeind* (*An Enemy of the People*), Schauspiel Dortmund, Dortmund, Germany, 2021. Photo: Birgit Hupfeld

Among the theaters in Germany, Denmark, and other European countries, which our project investigated and accompanied, the Betty Nansen Teatret and Schauspiel Dortmund went furthest in turning curatorial declarations of intents into actual, material production modes and concrete dramaturgic action. Powers are here no longer just symbolically renegotiated; instead privileges factually get redistributed. These theaters' institutional dramaturgies, whether performed by designated dramaturgs or others, are centrally involved with the reshaping of the theaters' self-positioning within their cities and communities, with actually facilitating the access and participation for diverse artists and art forms, and with renegotiating the institutions' cultural ownership with the public and developing with audiences new critical optics commensurate with polyphonic and cocreative aesthetics through adult education classes or intensive social media engagement. They accompany and frame these ventures into new institutional territories, demonstrating dramaturgic attentiveness to the real-life conflicts that emerge, and how these are articulated and navigated. Theater dramaturgy thus gets challenged to demonstrate that beyond its ability to curate enticing new profiles, stories and images of diversity and plurality, its actual, manifest skills of organizing agonistic communication can indeed make a difference in leading deep systemic postrepresentational transformations—nourishing the hope that they will not end in the tragic catastrophe some see on the horizon *because of*, others due to *a lack of*, such fundamental institutional changes as they characterize the present European theater landscape.

NOTES

1. Nora Sternfeld, "Inside the Post-representative Museum," in *Contemporary Curating and Museum Education*, ed. Carmen Mörsch, Angeli Sachs, and Thomas Sieber (Bielefeld, Germany: transcript, 2016), 175–86.

2. Julia Wissert and Christopher-Fares Köhler, "Let's Talk about Diversity: Moving beyond Representation and into the Difficult Structures of Change" (lecture), Aarhus, Denmark, May 28, 2021.

3. Wissert and Köhler, "Let's Talk about Diversity."

4. Viktoria Göke, interview with the author, Dortmund, June 7, 2024.

5. Julia Wissert, interview with the author, Dortmund, June 7, 2024.

6. Till Briegleb, "Die verschleierte Diva: Das Publikum, die ewige große Unbekannte, und vagabundierende Interessenswolken," in *Theater Heute: Das Jahrbuch 2023* (Berlin: Der Theaterverlag, 2023), 18–22, quotation on 22; my translation.

7. Wissert, interview with the author, June 7, 2024.

8. Julia Wissert, "Get Comfortable with the Uncomfortable," lecture at the debate Art of Assembly 27: The Arts as Playground for the Urban White Middle Class, Aarhus, March 19 2024, https://art-of-assembly.net/material/julia-wissert/ 4:13, 6:33.

9. Wissert, "Get Comfortable with the Uncomfortable."

10. Lisa Kraglund and Agnes Norlin Engvén, research dossier "Betty Nansen Teatret," including unpublished email interview with Eva Præstiin, MA in dramaturgy, Aarhus University, December 2023.

11. Kat Sekjær, "At Udvikle scenekunst af høj kvalitet i kollektive processer kræver tid til at teste og fejle: Interview med Eva Præstiin," *Applaus*, May 6, 2021, https://applaus.nu /nyheder/eva-praestiin-at-udvikle-scenekunst-af-hoj-kvalitet/.

12. *Eight Paths to Collective Co-creation*, Betty Nansen Teatret, May 23, 2023, https:// bettynansen.dk/betty-udvikler/8-paths-to-collective-co-creation-at-the-betty-nansen -theater/.

13. Sekjær, "At Udvikle scenekunst."

14. Wissert, interview with the author, June 7, 2024.

15. "Manifest: Flerstemmigt—Fysisk—Feministisk," Betty Nansen Teatret, January 9, 2024, https://bettynansen.dk/betty-udvikler/manifest-flerstemmigt-fysisk-feministisk/.

16. Kraglund and Norlin Engvén, research dossier.

17. Elsa Keslassy, "Danish Industry Addresses Structural Racism, Lack of Diversity in Movies, TV Series," *Variety*, March 7, 2023, https://variety.com/2023/film/global/danish -industry-structural-racism-a-bigger-picture-1235542183/.

18. Regarding Anna Bergmann, see Sally Mcgrane, "At This Theater, All of the Directors Will Be Women," *New York Times*, September 27, 2018, https://www.nytimes.com/2018 /09/27/theater/female-directors.html.

Alessandra Seutin's
Mimi's Shebeen, KVS,
Brussels, Belgium,
2023. Courtesy of
KVS

Kopano Maroga

Disruptive Dramaturgies

White Institutions, Black Agendas, and the Pursuit

of Dramaturgical Agency

The limited possibility that institutions in the European arts and cultural sector may offer spaces for a critical and potentially radical politics has, for me, never been more clearly articulated than in the aftermath of the attacks in occupied Palestine on October 7, 2023. This moment was dominated by responses ranging from overwhelmingly tepid to downright oppressive from this same arts and culture sector in the face of the ongoing Palestinian liberation struggle. I say this knowing full well that the possibility of radical politics in these spaces has always been less of a possibility and more of an impossible desire: a desire rooted in a personal kind of postcolonial malaise that hopes for a kind of impossible solidarity from supposedly previous colonial superpowers. Such a solidarity is impossible because it would guarantee the end of the dominance of these so-called superpowers, a reneging of the mechanisms of neocolonial domination that allow for the maintenance of said dominance: development economics, widespread military occupation in the Global South by nations of the Global North, the assassination of democratically elected leaders in the Global South with an anti-imperial agenda, and so on, and so on. And as Assata Shakur so soberly and somberly reminds us in *Assata: An Autobiography*, "Nobody in the world, nobody in history, has ever gotten their freedom by appealing to the moral sense of the people who were oppressing them."[1] For me, this overarching political context of the material reality of ongoing Western imperialism is the only framework that helps me think through and understand the dynamics of European cultural institutions and my place in them as a subject of the Global South (namely South Africa). But I'm getting ahead of myself. Let me introduce myself and map out what I'm going to try to do here, with these words on these pages.

My name is Kopano Maroga. I'm a Black South African cultural worker, who worked as an institutional dramaturg from 2019 to 2023 at Kunstencentrum VIERNUL-

Theater 55:2 DOI 10.1215/01610775-11683494

VIER in Ghent, Belgium. In my time at VIERNULVIER (an institution where, at the time of my employ, I was the only sub-Saharan African Black person on a fixed contract of a team of roughly ninety-five employees) I was exposed to all manner of everyday racisms and political inconsistencies. One day it was the casual use of the *n*-word from my white then–artistic director (which harks back to the racism experiences of Black German theater actress Maya Alban-Zapata while working with the State Theater an der Parkaue in Germany), the next it was the insistence on working with dance companies with a known record of harmful relationships with their employees.[2] And so the period of being house dramaturg forced me to contend with whether I would be the continual killjoy (à la Sara Ahmed), or whether I would keep my head down and not rock the boat in order to maintain my residence in the country, which was dependent on my employment with the institution. A postcolonial conundrum. In the end, I decided to speak out publicly about the harm I had experienced in the institution (sexual harassment and racism) as well as the alleged abuses taking place in dance companies with which we as an institution were affiliated, namely Rosas of Anne Terese de Keersmaeker (a well-established contemporary dance company) and Voetvolk of Lisbeth Gruwez (ironically, Gruwez is a graduate of the contemporary dance school PARTS, founded by de Keersmaeker). The response, after months of mediation with VIERNULVIER and my insistence on my right to articulate what had been and was still happening led to the end of my employment, which meant I had to leave the country soon after as well. I think this illustrates some of the inevitable postcolonial tensions that exist for those in the core(s) of empire trying to do critical work against imperial hegemony. And it is from this point of tension that I would like to think through the possibilities within this conundrum through conversation with a previous city dramaturg of the Koninklijke Vlaamse Schouwburg (KVS; the Royal Flemish Theatre) in Brussels, Belgium, Tunde Adefioye.

Adefioye is a Black American of Nigerian descent who worked as a city dramaturg for KVS between 2016 and 2019. His arrival in Belgium in 2007 saw him move from a PhD in chemo informatics at KU Leuven to founding a slam poetry organization in 2009, Urban Woorden, which was awarded the Cultural Prize for cultural education in Flanders in 2013. We met over an unstable internet connection on Google Meets to discuss the shaky ground of Black agendas and Black agency in the face of the colonial, consumptive desire of predominantly white, European institutions.

INSTITUTIONAL CONSUMPTION AND CAPTIVE MATERNAL CARE

> The institution is going to do whatever it needs [to do] to continue to be "King of the Hill." And part of what it needs to do to remain "King of the Hill" is extract and consume . . . consume Black bodies, consume Black knowledge . . . consume critical thought. —Tunde Adefioye, in conversation with the author

When reflecting on his time as city dramaturg at KVS, Adefioye refers to the idea of consumption. We talk about the consumptive desire seemingly built into white institutions that propels their reach for the cultural production of Black people writ large, under the banner of diversity, equity, and inclusion. Adefioye reflects critically on the politics of representation in his article "Social Death on Parade" when he refers to those of us who are "dying to be seen," a play on words that gestures to a kind of necropolitics that emerges in the sphere of institutionalized cultural practice.[3] That the selfsame representation politics, an arrested and appropriated identity politics, that were so espoused by movements such as Black Lives Matter can facilitate the ground for the unmaking of the very people meant to benefit from said representation is an illustration of the insurgency of white colonial desire. To put it another way, when considering Audre Lorde's oft-quoted "The master's tools will never dismantle the master's house," what happens when we ourselves as people who desire and work toward the abolition of imperial terror embody said "master's tools"?

"I was actually put in service to do the master's work," Tunde Adefioye says. Adefioye reflects with me on a particular expedition he took to Nigeria under the banner of his work at KVS to do on-site research with a local Babalawo (a high priest of the traditional Yoruba religion) for the development of an artist of color's work who was in residence at KVS: "I look [back] at it now...almost four years later and...it was almost nothing but extraction....We were all racialized people, but, actually, at the end of the day...we [were] reproducing some of the same things that we [find] ourselves critiquing."

Malcolm X., Jr.cE.sA.r (Junior Mthombeni, Cesar Janssens, and Fikry El Azzouzi), KVS, Stadsschouwburg Utrecht, Utrecht, Netherlands, 2019. Courtesy of KVS

Specifically, Adefioye lodges the critique at himself, as opposed to the artist who has a long-standing relationship with the Babalawo. In his self-critique I hear a reflection on his role as the quasi emissary of the white institution—an echo of the colonial strategy of control of cherry-picking so-called Native elites who proved sympathetic and/or useful to the colonial agenda and elevating them to a stratum of social and political power that would allow the colonial masters to rule the Native territory in absentia. In this instance, it is Adefioye's race and ethnicity that open the door for the European institutions' "extraction in absentia," which is concurrently complicated by the sincere desire to work with African epistemologies espoused by Africans themselves. And this desire is ultimately undermined by the fact that the work gets presented back in Europe for a predominantly European audience. It's not my intention to say that this kind of knowledge exchange is without merit or mutual benefit; rather, I want to highlight how the pathways of production follow the old colonial trajectories of imperial extraction from the South for consumption in the North. And as Adefioye points out, "We have to make sure we spend enough time and resources...creating enough care. Care for ourselves, care of each other and care of...our lineage." It is at this juncture of conflicted caretaking that Dr. Joy James's notion of the "Captive Maternal" becomes especially operationable. James, a Black American political philosopher, describes Captive Maternals' function as follows:

> Captive maternals are self-identified female, male, trans or ungendered persons feminized and socialized into caretaking within the legacy of racism and US democracy. Captive maternals are designated for consumption in the tradition of chattel slavery; they stabilize with their labor the very social and state structures which prey upon them....
>
> The captive maternal labors to nurture the "private realm" of family and community that seek shelter from social and state aggression and stabilize the "public realm" of policing, presidential powers and policies that prey upon said family and community. An anti-black (inter)national Womb steals or appropriates the generative powers of captive maternals in order to stabilize the state and social order. Their desperate needs to stabilize black families and communities lead to "pragmatic" negotiations of labor and loyalty that lead to conformity to prevailing norms: capitalism; two-party electoral system; subservience to hegemony and dominant racial/gender/sexual/ideological elites.[4]

James proceeds to expand on the five stages of the Captive Maternal: the Conflicted or Celebrated Caretaker, the Protestor, the Movement Maker, the Maroon/Marronage, and, finally, the War Resistor. The stage of the Conflicted Caretaker is of particular interest in discussing Black institutional cultural workers such as institutional dramaturgs. James writes of this stage, "Survival under captivity requires or dictates compromises."[5] For institutional dramaturgs who hold an antiracist and/or anti-imperialist politic and/or desire, working within predominantly white, European structures that represent capital accumulation via the legacies of racial capitalism and imperial extraction poses glaring contradictions—contradictions that are, in the first instance, mostly navigated via compromise. We compromise our politics to meet our and our communities' material needs (such as an income) and the possibility of supporting communities of color through our presence in these institutions; we stabilize with our labor the very institutions that prey on us and render our discourses of rebellion and revolution into inert art objects and art moments; by our mere presence(s), we validate the (seemingly implicit) antiracist image of the institutions in which we serve.

During our conversation, Adefioye reflects on a particular instance of his work as the city dramaturg of KVS that reflects the contradictions of the Conflicted Caretaker. In 2018, Adefioye invited Kenyan theater-maker Ogutu Muraya to present his work *Fractured Memories* as part of a decolonization focus program at KVS. Unbeknownst to Muraya, his work would be featured alongside a revival of Hugo Claus's 1970 *Het leven en de werken van Leopold II* (*The Life and Works of Leopold II*), directed by Raven Ruëll. The work was marketed as a satirical portrait of Leopold II and Belgium's colonial history. However, after seeing the use of blackface, racial slurs, and racial stereotyping in the play, Muraya made the decision to pull out of presenting his work, explaining in a public statement,

> It is with a heavy heart that I cancelled my performances at KVS in Brussels. I fail to understand and justify why KVS felt the need to produce and stage a piece that inferiorizes black people in the most derogatory and disrespectful ways possible, in the name of using satire to criticize a genocidal maniac—Leopold II. I fail to understand and justify the use racist slurs e.g. nigger, apish characterization, imbecilic mannerisms, racialized costumes, sexualization of black body, black face, colonial mentality and many more problematic devices in the portrayal of black people. I fail to understand and justify how such a work can be produced and staged by KVS in the name of decolonization. I fail to understand and justify why my work is programmed next to such a hyper-problematic piece and described and framed without my consent as being part of the same conversation to "reflect critically on our colonial past..." I fail to understand and justify why I was not asked or consulted in connection with this framing. I fail to understand and justify why I should perform at all at KVS in such a contemptuous context.[6]

In response to Muraya's cancellation, along with a series of other critical reflections from other writers,[7] Adefioye offered a public apology to the maker and to those who had seen the work and felt betrayed and offended by the theater's choice.[8] "I just thought it was my responsibility actually to say something after this piece and after Ogutu had to then had to go through this," he told me.

In reflecting on his intervention and handling of the incident with Muraya, Adefioye exemplifies the Conflicted Caretaker at work. His attempt to reconcile the backlash of the racist work commissioned by his colleagues and cosigned by artistic director of KVS, Michael de Cock, by apologizing in his own name is a gesture of potential care

Malcolm X.,
Jr.cE.sA.r (Junior
Mthombeni, Cesar
Janssens, and Fikry
El Azzouzi), KVS,
Stadsschouwburg
Utrecht, Utrecht,
Netherlands, 2019.
Courtesy of KVS

and accountability. However, given his role as city dramaturg of the same institution, his apology can come across as a de facto apology on behalf of the institution; such an apology seems misplaced, and in fact the KVS team discouraged Adefioye from relaying it. The optics of the senior-most Black employee of a predominantly white institution apologizing for the racist artistic choices of the same institution's white employees is a painful example of the contradictions inherent in trying to negotiate critical Black cultural participation in a field dominated by whiteness. Tangentially, I think here of the widely circulated image of the Black American ambassador to the United Nations, Linda Thomas-Greenfield, raising her hand to veto a resolution for an immediate ceasefire in Gaza after the October 7 attacks in occupied Palestine—an illustration that speaks to how elites of color are leveraged in service of the agenda of their respective empires.

In a public response to Adefioye's and others' criticism about the staging of *Het leven en de werken van Leopold II*, De Cock shared that the work had been presented in Kinshasa and Matongé in the Democratic Republic of the Congo since its premiere in 2003, to much success. He also said that it was a shame that those critical of the piece were not able to pick up on the work's satire, then asked whether, in the context of the critical spirit around the piece, art is still free.[9] Though De Cock's response might itself be characterized as a work of satire, it highlights something potentially instructive about the politics of relation surrounding racial politics in white institutions: white institutions can seemingly autonomously and arbitrarily decide what does and does not constitute racism. No amount of opposition by critical voices of color would be sufficient to stand against this near-absolute power in meaning making. And it is in this terrain that cultural workers of color are invited to offer critique—not for the purposes of challenging hegemonic orders of meaning making and material dominance (such as coloniality) and how these may materialize in institutional cultural work but, rather, to function as objects that can *comment* on materiality but are denied from *affecting* materiality. They effectively serve as vehicles for discourses on struggles against imperial and racial violence to remain *discursive* as opposed to *operationable*. Further, calling for the dramaturgical insights of a Black dramaturg into a predominantly white institution and then subsequently undermining their racial critique of the organization itself seems to be a tactic of imperial dominance, a classic bait and switch: the problem is not that the work is racist, it is that *you* who critique the work do not have the intellectual refinement to appreciate its satire. The problem of racism is not a problem of white violence; it is a problem of people of color's inability to understand. As Adefioye concludes,

> When this work [*Het leven en de werken van Leopold II*] was presented . . . and this is where the tokenization comes in, my response should not have been, "Oh, this is a problematic piece, let's definitely ask someone who has a much, much better and much more . . . relevant understanding of the colonial legacy [to present their work alongside it]." . . . That should not have been my response. My response should have been, like, "No, we are not going to do this," and "Not in my name." . . . So then . . . this was not my purpose in [2018], but Ogutu's piece then becomes instrumentalized by the institution thanks to me.

I suppose, then, the next question would be, "What is to be done?" Adefioye refers to the idea of "stealing away," borrowed from Fred Moten and Stefano Harney's *The Undercommons: Fugitive Planning and Black Study*:

> If one were to insist, the opposite of professionalization is that fugitive impulse to rely on the undercommons for protection, to rely on the honor, and to insist on the honor of the fugitive community; if one were to insist, the opposite of professionalization is that criminal impulse to steal from professions, from the university, with neither apologies nor malice, to steal the enlightenment for others, to steal oneself with a certain blue music, a certain tragic optimism, to steal away with mass intellectuality; if one were to do this, would this not be to place criminality and negligence against each other?[10]

Adefioye insists on the inevitability of tokenization in white institutions for their employees of color, and, as a potential mitigating factor, speaks to the necessity for nondominant communities to invest in practices of reappropriating resources for the purposes of the stabilization and support of their communities: stealing away.

The largely anecdotal accounts shared above are not sufficient to analyze a field as broad as racial relations in white, European institutions. I do believe, however, there is something to be learned from our stories as cultural workers opposed to imperialism, and the resonances these stories share in the limited scope that white, European institutions have in dealing with imperial violence in their own institutions, with the broader, macropolitical framework of ongoing Western imperialism. I honestly cannot say whether these racial relations are improving via inclusion of nonwhite and anti-imperial voices and perspectives or worsening by the assimilation of these same voices into an impotent politics that *represents* change but is denied from *affecting* material change. Moreover, the very question of whether European cultural institutions can be anti-imperial poses contradictions, given that the foundations and funding structures that allow for these institutions to exist are either linked to a colonial history (whether directly or indirectly) or benefit from the contemporary global neocolonial relations that continue the tradition of mass extraction from the Global South for consumption and the upholding of the Global North's global dominance. That said, I believe that, as Moten and Harney argue, those with an anti-imperial desire within colonially descended and proximate institutions need to identity their "fugitive community."[11] There is a need for us to engage in deep, collective study toward articulating an anti-imperial politics and praxis that speak to the specific challenges we face, that can itself reach out and contribute to the broader community and movement of institutional fugitivity.

Notes

1. Assata Shakur, *Assata: An Autobiography* (Chicago: Lawrence Hill Books, 1987), 151.

2. Katharina Schmidt, "Keine Bühne für Rassismus," *Die Tagezseitung*, June 30, 2019, https://taz.de/Rassismus-am-Theater/!5603768/.

3. Tundé Adefioye, "Social Death on Parade," *Rektoverso.be*, August 31, 2022, https://www.rektoverso.be/artikel/social-death-on-parade.

4. Joy James, "Captive Maternals: Sally, Michelle, and Deborah," *Abolition Journal* (blog), June 29, 2020, https://abolitionjournal.org/presidential-powers-and-captive-maternals-sally-michelle-and-deborah/.

5. Joy James, "The Captive Maternal Is a Function, Not an Identity Marker," *Scalawag*, April 28, 2023, https://scalawagmagazine.org/2023/04/captive-maternal-joy-james/.

6. Veem House of Performance, "Ogutu Muraya about the Cancellation of His Performances at KVS Brussels," Facebook, March 18, 2018, https://www.facebook.com/veem.house/posts/1206457946153437/.

7. Margot Luyckfasseel, Naomi Ntakiyica, and Nora Mahammed, "Beste Raven, slechte timing!," *Rektoverso.be*, March 13, 2018, https://www.rektoverso.be/artikel/beste-raven-slechte-timing; Charlotte De Somviele, "KVS Struikelt over Leopold II-Voorstelling uit 2003," *De Standaard*, March 10, 2018, https://www.standaard.be/cnt/dmf20180309_03401369.

8. Tundé Adefioye, "Lachen met een moordzuchtige Maniak," *De Standaard*, March 13, 2018, https://www.standaard.be/cnt/dmf20180312_03405958.

9. Adefioye, "Lachen met een moordzuchtige Maniak."

10. Stefano Harney and Fred Moten, *The Undercommons: Fugitive Planning and Black Study* (Wivenhoe, UK: Minor Compositions, 2013), https://www.minorcompositions .info/wp-content/uploads/2013/04/undercommons-web.pdf.

11. Harney and Moten, *The Undercommons*, 40.

Dea Loher's
Ms. Yamamoto
Is Still There,
Schauspielhaus
Zürich, Zurich,
Switzerland, 2024.
Photo: Alex Bunge

Panel

"Some Institutions Are More Horizontal Than Others"

This panel discussion took place in hybrid form during the Performance Studies international (PSi) annual conference in London, on June 21, 2024. The idea was to bring theater practitioners, scholars, and dramaturgs together in conversation to identify challenges and discuss transformations currently underway across various European city- and state-funded theaters. As a result of recent activist momentum (and artistic direction scandals!), European public theaters are currently being held accountable for structural inequality, power abuse, racism, and sexism, resulting in a moment of reckoning and reassessment that inspired our panel discussion. In the conversation below, our expert panelists were able to report on the situation of theater institutions across various national contexts.

As a starting point, we looked at the move toward more horizontal and democratic institutional cultures dating back to the late 1960s in the German and Flemish contexts, which resulted in a recognition of issues of class and minoritarian identities, respectively. On the other hand, the radical equality enshrined in the Norwegian theater context has actually constituted a challenge for artistic freedoms, articulating a tension between democratic structures and artistic processes. The discussion also explored the colonial legacy that has yet *to be fully accounted for in the French and Belgian contexts. As such, it continues to have implications for Afropean artists struggling for recognition and is perpetuated in the tokenization of guest artists from the African continent. Adding to the nuance of the discussion was how the activist momentum of postcolonial discourse resonates differently from the postmigrant discourse, opening distinct avenues of activism within different national contexts. The term* postmigrant *potentially enables us to go one step further: to recognize the "native/migrant" binary as false and instead to perceive human societies as always already shaped by migration.*

Our discussion was to a large extent framed by concrete examples of current challenges and, at the same time, signs of progress in European public theater. It succinctly delineated how our panel assesses the current situation and what they hope to see undertaken in the years to come. If there is one unifying thread through the conversation, it would be the panelists' urgent appeal for openness and transparency that needs to accompany processes of democratization and diversification.

This conversation has been edited for clarity and concision.

—Christine Korte

Theater 55:2 DOI 10.1215/01610775-11683507

LILY CLIMENHAGA *I'd like to first of all thank everyone on this beautiful panel for joining us today. We're going to move in different temporalities through some important questions within contemporary theaters, so we're going to start with a backward gaze. Looking at the past into the present, starting with two fabulous scholars on our panel: Noah Lena and Anna.*

NOAH LENA VERCAUTEREN I'm researching Flanders and the Netherlands, and it's interesting, because when we think about institutional dramaturgy, about theater institutions and their history, we often have this typical philosophy around nationalism, national identity, and community in mind. This is harder to apply to Flanders and the Netherlands, because it's a small area where there aren't

Olga Mouak in Eva Doumbia's *Le iench*, La Part du Pauvre, CDN de Normandie-Rouen, Rouen, France, 2020. Photo: Arnaud Berterau

actually a lot of famous playwrights. Our cultural tradition when it comes to our language is pretty small. If you had a week off, you'd probably be able to read all of the most famous Dutch-speaking playwrights. So when you talk about repertoire, when you talk about the cultural theater tradition, you get a lot of different answers in this area, where every institution has to almost invent a new tradition and a new repertoire.

There have also been two cultural movements that have changed how these institutions function. One is a wave of democratization and counterinstitutional movements that started in the Netherlands and moved to Flanders. It started with Aktie Tomaat, translated as "Action Tomato." In 1969, a couple of new actors wanted to open a discussion by throwing tomatoes at a restaging in Amsterdam of *The Tempest*. What followed were a number of open debates that left a lot of theater-makers very dissatisfied, who then started forming theater collectives outside of institutions.

These collectives were founded with a completely horizontal philosophy in mind. Everyone was doing everything. This method and the resulting productions were doing really well, which the institutions noticed. Starting in the 1980s, there were also a lot of aesthetic changes in Flanders specifically, due to the success of the Flemish wave. Flemish theater-makers, choreographers, and directors were breaking the boundaries of theater and performance and were deconstructing classic drama. They were gaining popularity internationally, which made their work and their way of working all the more popular in Flanders. This in turn meant that the institutions had to start looking again at these "margins" of experimental theater, just as they had done with the theater collectives in the 1970s.

So in comparison with other nations, there is this history in the Netherlands and Flanders of theater from the margins growing more and more popular, eventually taking the center, and the institutions trying to follow these movements because they have to continuously invent their own traditions anyway.

CLIMENHAGA *Let's pass the ball to Anna.*

ANNA VOLKLAND I'll begin by telling you a bit about the German history of challenging theater institutions in the postwar, post-Nazi era. The reopened, often hierarchical German state and city theaters were mainly still organized like during the Nazis' time—with one charismatic leader on top. After the war, theaters were one of the first organizations built back up. The idea was that theaters—which had actually worked quite well during the Nazi era—should now be places of "rehumanization" and "reeducation for democracy." This idea of theater as a place for "democracy" lived on in both East and West Germany but took different paths.

Now I'm going to jump to the 1960s. Noah Lena mentioned the Action Tomato in Belgium. In 1969, at the same time, in West Germany, Willy Brandt claimed, "We want to dare more democracy," and there was a larger wish, desire, demand to democratize established institutions like universities and theaters—to fight the old authoritarian ways of thinking. This demand came from left-wing (nonparliamentary) political groups and the students' movement but was also present in society. The most important focus for the demands for more "diversity" (though the term wasn't used) and democratization was the "class issue" and the associated social injustice. So, at this time, we had this call for the democratization of working structures: the idea that actors were the "workers of the theater," the exploited ones. They recognized an obvious contradiction: while actors could (and should) demand *freedom* onstage, offstage their opinion wasn't worth too much. They couldn't decide *what* and often also *how* they wanted to play; they couldn't decide what costumes they wore, and so on. So the "fight for democratization" inside public theater institutions started with the actors as fundamental critics of power structures.

CLIMENHAGA *You talk about the democratization of these spaces, and I'm curious about the experiences of those working in theater today. Do you see there still being a legacy of democratization? Do you see this opening up of a conversation around who gets to make the choices, who's doing the labor, and where the labor belongs?*

MARIANA ARISTIZÁBAL I can share my experience working in different institutions. I guess the answer is that it depends on size. When the institution is really small and overworked, it feels more democratic, because it feels like the workload is shared, because everyone needs to hold the space, whereas in bigger institutions, there is a really strict hierarchy that's very hard to break, because it has been established and has been in place for many, many, many years. What I find interesting is our resistance, as humans, to change: a fear of change. It also depends on the type of institution and the level of the project. When it's a really big, large-scale project with—I don't know—over twenty-five performers and a creative team of over forty people, it becomes harder to have those conversations and make that democratic space. So, just for the sake of time, it becomes more hierarchical.

KOPANO MAROGA I come from a dance background in live art performance, with some experience in theater and text. For the past four years—until last year—I worked as a dramaturg at a Flemish institution, VIERNULVIER (previously Vooruit), that really prides itself on its democratization and horizontality. So, building off what Noah Lena said about the Flemish scene and the integration of more horizontal models, you see this idea quite often in institutions. This hierarchy is so ingrained that somehow it becomes enmeshed within this idea of horizontality. It becomes a bit of an animal farm. And while some institutions are more horizontal than others, it's quite complex, because when we talk about democracy, we're talking about modernity.

I'm coming from a South African perspective, and when I was working in Europe, it was really hard to imagine that there was a disconnect with the presentation of African people—of Black people—in the twentieth century that extended into the twenty-first century. I'm talking about the human zoos and hyperethnographic, hyperexotic representations. Seemingly without investigation, we transitioned into a moment that claims to present the work of diverse people without considering the history it comes from. So when I think about democracy, I also think about human rights and the human rights charter, which was drafted in 1948—ironically, the same year that apartheid was drafted into law in South Africa and the Nakba took place in Palestine. So it indicates which people are considered human and which people are not.

The only African nation that signed the Charter of Human Rights was the Union of South Africa, its name back when it was predominantly represented by white men. This idea of democratization in European institutions is complicated because the twentieth-century idea of democracy is embedded in the extraction and exoticization of people from the Global South. When I arrived in Belgium, it was quite a strange situation, because there was this idea that, by virtue of my presence, there was some level of equality in terms of engagement. But I'm there as a foreign national, and every six months I have to go to the government and say, "Hey, please let me stay in the country. I promise I'm one of the good ones"—not something my colleagues have to do. How does that translate in terms of democratization? In the horizontalization of voices? I don't know how feasible this institutional frame is in a decolonial or postcolonial framework. In Ghent, the last human zoo didn't close until the 1960s. It's still in living memory, and yet there's not really engagement with it. As artists, how do we make sense of a history that suddenly shifts from exoticization to representation? In the twenty-first century, there's a necessity for diverse representation in these arts houses, which often leads to tokenization. But then again, the tokenization is not caused by ill will, right? It's part of the structure. When I arrived at the institution, I was the only Black person on the team, which, in 2019, I was like, "How?" But we know how: colonization.

YUVVIKI DIOH I was thinking about this question of democratization because how I experience this life and body within an institution is very—Kopano, what you just said is also true for Switzerland. Our human zoos also didn't close until the 1960s, and the University of Zurich had these conferences on very old, problematic racist theories. Nevertheless, from an organizational perspective, the outgoing artistic directors [Nicolas Stemann and Benjamin von Blomberg] prided themselves on trying to have this kind of horizontal leadership. They really tried to break up the hierarchization of decision-making. It doesn't mean that it always worked. It doesn't mean that they didn't make mistakes. For me, it was interesting to experience how messy democratization can be within an institution.

As the diversity agent, as one of the few Black people in the institution, as the first person to ever do this job in this house, suddenly I became leadership. Suddenly I became the one with power. Suddenly I'm responsible for a lot of things without really realizing what that meant. Additionally, I have the will and

the belief that we should do collective work, but in an institution of 350 people, collective work is really difficult. It is also connected with knowledge transfer. Right? It's really difficult to transmit knowledge. I don't understand the work of a light technician, but I need to find a way to speak with them in order to have these strategies and tools for democratization.

It's a very Swiss thing to talk about democracy, and it's something that a lot of people here have an access to. But you realize that there are a lot of different, let's say, motivations for it. You encounter people who want to be part of decision-making for their own career purposes. You also have the case where a lot of people are deeply embedded or rooted in theories of democratization that are themselves rooted in white perspectives, male perspectives. Complexity is a big thing when you try to democratize an institution and you do have these questions of responsibility. People sometimes really want leadership, like really authoritarian leadership, where I also wonder: How? Why?

JULIAN BLAUE I agree. While it's a difficult task to democratize theater work, I really believe in it and have for a long time. I also believe in theater as a model for society, uniting practical, intellectual, and artistic work. But living in a country like Norway, which is famous for its equality and horizontal structures, which has one of the world's oldest democratic constitutions and the *Jantelov* (Jante law)—which means we are all equal (a very popular moral in Norway, by the way)—it sometimes makes theater work nearly impossible. For example, workers have very good rights, but it's not Beuys's vision that all humans are artists; instead it's more that all artists are just people. Often, when I work in those institutions, the workers' rights are so strong that they can destroy the artistic process. If you want to light a cigarette onstage, they can say no, even if there are important artistic reasons to do so. For example, Vegard Vinge and Ida Müller just worked here and are really big stars in continental Europe. They come from Norway originally (Vinge is Norwegian, Müller German-Norwegian) but are sometimes almost treated like nobodies at the theaters here, which makes their performances sometimes almost impossible to realize, because everybody has so many rights, but not everyone has an understanding of artistic processes. So I think democratization has a

limit, even if I, from a political standpoint, really believe in it.

CLIMENHAGA *Olga, I'm interested in your perspective as both an actor and somebody creating their own production in a landscape that's had some pretty significant financial cuts lately.*

OLGA MOUAK As Anna was talking about the idea of power to the workers, I suddenly felt very French, because we have such a strong tradition of unionizing, because we have this very industrial past of mining culture. Lately, talking about the conditions of the miners in the old coal mines and the political consequences of closing those mines is coming back in trend, because it created a sense of abandonment and led people to embrace political ideas that were not really what the worker and the union spirit was about. Because of this strong worker past, class and the rich/poor divide are understood. However, we still struggle with notions of race.

Returning to what was said earlier about hierarchies in theaters, in France, we have big, prestigious houses. For example, Comédie-Française, which is basically Molière's company: its aim is to conserve the heritage of Molière and the traditional repertoire. There the technicians are revered and respected. They have contracts, and the French system makes it pretty difficult for someone with a long-standing contract to be evicted from the institution. We have a lot of workers' rights, but it can be very different if you work as a freelancer. It remains very segmented. It's still technicians with technicians, actors with actors, and producers with producers. Sometimes as an actor, you can navigate this whole landscape of people, but there are often communication issues between creators and technicians. As Julian was saying, sometimes the friction is so strong that it can create huge dif-

Guido Garcia Lueches's *Playing Latinx*, Soho Theatre, London, 2024. Photo: Charly Monreal

ficulties for the creative process. But there is also friction between production and artists, because most of the time you have a vision, and you want to go for it, and someone has to say, "Yeah, there's no money."

Returning to tokenism, I'm mostly fascinated to see how I thought we were making progress. Yet now I have this feeling that we're going backwards because of the political climate and the fact that the money for subsidized theaters isn't only coming from the Ministry of Culture—which is, at the moment, centrist—it's also coming from municipalities, where the extreme right is overpowering everyone. Even a festival like Avignon, which is a well-known, famous festival, is struggling because they're surrounded by right-wing extremists. So, it's a progression in terms of diversity, but a political context working against it.

CLIMENHAGA *Perhaps this is a good space to move into the question of what is happening in these institutions. What needs to happen? What isn't happening?*

MAROGA For context, I had a very violent expulsion from my previous employment because I started speaking publicly about internal racism and sexual harassment, as well as about the harm taking place more broadly in the sector. I'd taught for quite a while at P.A.R.T.S., the contemporary dance school in Brussels, and from my students there was a lot of information about harm taking place in the school and the company. The number one thing that needs to happen or is missing is, we need to disabuse ourselves of the fetishization of democracy. I think there's something about the democratic model that is so interwoven with white supremacist capitalist culture at this particular juncture that we haven't really analyzed. There's this dream of democracy

that represents society and ourselves as the best version of ourselves, but I think, as Julian was saying, there are certain practical realities imposed by bureaucracy that actually impede the possibility of engaging with one another democratically. Like Julian was talking about, the power of workers and how that overpowers the artistic vision. And Olga mentioned something similar in terms of hyperunionization, which means that the possibility of thinking outside the box is limited. It's very neoliberal to have the primary objective of art to be to exist in perpetuity. It's not necessarily about creating art. It's not necessarily about representation. It's about what gets prioritized in terms of funding. I mean this quite economically, having been inside an organization and seeing what goes into a policy plan, a federal funding application. It's ironic, you know, to say that we serve artists, but the majority of the budget goes to the building and the staff.

Something that is happening is a kind of perversion of radical politics. So, despite institutions adopting diversity with aesthetics, language, and semi-integration, they are still predominantly represented by the charismatic white male head, who is a liaison for government funding. Like Olga was saying, we take a step back, even though we take the step forward. "Okay, cool, there are Black people on the stage, there are disabled people on the stage, and we're talking about feminism!" But the director is a white man, and that white man goes and speaks to the government and gets or doesn't get the money. There just isn't a shared collective discourse about the situation as it is, as opposed to the situation we would like it to be. There's a necessity for candor, which is different from honesty. It's not that you have to tell me everything, but you don't need to lie to me. A lot of these institutions blatantly lie about their intentions, what their priorities are. I understand why. You need to get your funding. It's just to say that this idea of supporting artists is completely undermined by our economic reality, and there isn't an acknowledgment of what creates these hierarchies because apparently we're all democratic. It doesn't allow for dissent. If you dissent, you're villainized. So I think that we need to open space for that duplicity. Not necessarily to say, "Now we're going to solve the situation," but to have a level of candor and say, "Yes, we are entrenched and surrounded by far-right extremists. Yes, the money we get is dependent on how much we can perform a certain level of discipline in relation to that kind of far right political ideology." But you go into these theaters, and you see their mission and values are about egalitarianism, but that's not the reality of the majority-white, majority-able-bodied institution. I'm not saying that it's the institution's fault; I'm saying it's structural.

CLIMENHAGA *Mariana, what's this been like post-Brexit?*

ARISTIZÁBAL I was just thinking about what is and isn't happening in the UK. I think in terms of institutions: what I found in the last couple of years is that all of the institutions want to be on the right side of history. So they're trying desperately to prove that they are now hiring more diverse performers and diversifying the workforce. However, I find that we need to keep digging to get out of the pit we're in. Everyone is so desperate to try to get it right that they're not really truthful about their intentions. What they're doing feels incredibly tokenistic. I find myself in positions where I've become kind of like the representative of the oppressed without necessarily wanting to be that person. Suddenly I'm the voice of reason and experience, which I never asked to be. I was just asking to be another creative in the room. Institutions are really trying to have

these conversations and trying to implement things to hold these difficult spaces, and I think that's a great thing, but I feel that not everyone within institutions is aware of the need for these changes. I think institutions are made of people. They're not just an establishment. The people who work in these institutions are what make the institution. So if the people inside the institution don't understand why those changes are needed, if you take all of these bias and racial trainings to people who do not feel it is necessary, then there's no point. If it doesn't become part of the culture, this desire to learn about one another and see the other as an equal, then we're lacking.

VERCAUTEREN I think there's really something to that idea that so many people want to say, "We're democratized, we did racial training, so we can do it all." It's the legacy of that enlightenment humanist thinking where you believe, "If I just think long enough, me, myself, I'll get it. I'll understand as much as someone's lived experience." A lot of the initiatives that try to open up the institutions, they have good intentions, and I think in certain cases they do work. But it's also about the willingness to step back and to practice active listening. And when you introduce people in your institution, to have that be an active process and not just be like, "Here's your chair, sit in it, at our table." You have to be radical in it. But it's very hard for a lot of people because they just can't get into the philosophy of "I'm the problem and I'm going to have to sit with that." You're not going to be able to solve the problem in a lot of cases, you're not going to be that person. You can be a facilitator, if you're part of an institution. But the way Descartes wrote about it, "being master of nature" or whatever, you're not going to be that. I think it's letting go of that way of thinking that's really necessary.

Blaue & Poppy's
Death of Theatre, Birth of Law?,
in front of the Norwegian Parliament, Det Norske Teatret, Oslo, Norway, 2023.
Photo: Nikolai Bergstrøm

MOUAK Whenever I hear racial sensitivity training, I'm like, LOL. We don't have that in France. It's not a topic. In the French institution, we just started implementing sexual harassment training. It is mandatory for theaters to have one spokesperson who attends the workshop and returns to the institution to deliver what they learn. In a country with a reputation of protecting sexual harassers, this was a big deal, but racial sensitivity is not yet a thing. I was thinking about what needs to be done and what we don't see. In the French theater system, when we talk about diversity—I think when I first started working in theater, I understood diversity in its English or American meaning. I thought diversity means more diverse people, but then I realized in the French system—I don't know about the rest of Europe—they mean diversity of creation, not diversity of creators. What they really mean is to try to have as many women and men. It's not really about background or skin color. It's more about the diversity of what you offer as an artist.

We continue to struggle with the colonial past. There's still an absolute refusal to acknowledge the terrible consequences of colonization. In France, it's really a no-no subject. We don't talk about it. If you raise the problem, you become the problem. I feel like the institutions have found a way around it which is—I mean, young people would say it's cringe. And it really is in the sense that there is a distinction to be made between African artists from the former colonies who come to France for shows. In France, a lot of dancers from Western Africa are programmed in festivals and at big institutions. But they're not the same as Afropeans, people like me who were born in France to immigrant parents. Talking to the heads of many different institutions, the discourse is, "Well, look, you're complaining about racism and the lack of diversity, but you see those dancers from Ivory Coast? They're not complaining! They're very happy to be in the program. So what's your problem? What's your issue?" You have, on the one hand, the grateful ex-colonial artist who is just happy to showcase their work—often amazing work, by the way. On the other side, you have those unsatisfied, ungrateful Afropean artists who are always looking for things to criticize. I

Mouak in Eva Doumbia's *Autophagies*, La Part du Pauvre, Festival d'Avignon, Avignon, France, 2017. Photo: Armand Gauz

think this is what's missing for me, more of those perspectives onstage.

There was a big scandal at the last Avignon festival because an artist named Rébecca Chaillon presented a wonderful piece called *Carte noir nommée désir*. It made people so angry because she was basically presenting a work that made some people feel uncomfortable in its display of Black, female bodies and how it spoke about racism. They received a lot of hatred. The show was supposed to be shown in Odéon the next year, but one of the performers quit because she was harassed on the street while out with her baby. It's proof that these perspectives are needed, proof that they're being silenced because it's not the type of Black person you want to see or hear. It also accompanies this conversation on tokenism. Are you really sincere in the way that you want to create better work, or are you more interested in the makeup of it all? Like, am I cosplaying openness? This ques-

tion becomes even more interesting when you consider how France now has this law where half of the heads of artistic institutions have to be women, which is also present in the programming of festivals like Avignon. There Tiago Rodrigues was expected to have at least two female creatives featured in the two main venues. And he's doing it. It's happening, but it's an issue for some reason. It's like somehow there are no female artists. So in France, we have to go to Spain and find Angélica Liddell—who doesn't identify as a feminist, by the way.

BLAUE I couldn't agree more with Mariana and Olga. On the one hand, you have this ideology of being correct, being on the correct side of history, which from another point of view is a total luxurious problem to criticize, because of course it is a good thing to want to be on the correct side of history. At the theater I work at in Norway, I work with a POC theater director, and I think the Norwegian context is very similar to the German one, where the notion of postmigration makes more sense than the notion of postcolonialism. This point is especially interesting in theater. The concept of postmigrant theater was introduced in Germany by Shermin Langhof, a Turkish German director. The term is used to include a generation of Germans with migration backgrounds who referred to themselves as postmigrants. The term differentiated the current generation, with no direct migration experience, from that of their parents, who had themselves migrated to Germany. Simultaneously, there was no mainstream definition of postmigrant, thus this new generation had the possibility of defining it for themselves. But the term *postmigration* is even more interesting when used to highlight that every society is and always has been shaped by migration. Which, in turn, means there is, in fact, no such thing as an original people. We have always been shaped by migration. To answer the questions "What can we do?" and "What should theater institutions do?," I think we need to recognize that we are and always have been a postmigrant society. The question is not "if" but "how." Not if a society should be shaped by migration but how this can be done at its best. How to make migration become an institutional reality. I think the intention of trying to be more inclusive is an important ambition. But we have to dig even deeper, while still recognizing that the desire to be on the correct side of history is good and important.

VOLKLAND I just want to give a bit of hope regarding at least the question of democratization which we referred to as a quite problematic label that too often doesn't reflect all the ongoing exclusive practices and structures. I'll briefly jump to Thuringia, a small state in East Germany currently known for right-wing populism and the National Socialist Underground, so for Nazi crimes. But it's also home to Theaterhaus Jena. This very small theater was built after the end of the GDR [German Democratic Republic], post-1989. They founded Theaterhaus Jena with its special construction in the hopes of a really democratic way of working together—which again only means that all people involved in the theater work should ideally have the same opportunities to decide on and shape their way of being, working, creating together. The current artistic leadership team ("ensemble council") has been there for more than two years, and the whole theater just got an important theater prize for their ongoing attempts to *work together differently* and produce different kinds of theater—not so much for being "different" or "diverse" themselves. I think it maybe fulfills Julian's wishes as well, because in 1990–91 they began with a call for anarchy. They wanted, as much as possible, direct democracy—not a dictatorship and not bureaucracy; they'd already experienced that in the GDR.

Leon Pfannenmüller's *Blut*, Theaterhaus Jena, Jena, Germany, 2024. Photo: Joachim Dette

The technicians there and all those in nonartistic departments, those who make art possible, are equal to the artists. But still, they don't all do the same, because even though they are working together equally, in the end it's not equal; because the art, the theater production is the focus and some employees are closer to the artistic or programmatic decisions than others—which they are very open about. There's an openness about the process and the failures or limits.

CLIMENHAGA *In the last couple of years, partially because of Milo Rau, partially because of other theater houses like in Zurich, we have this concept of a city theater of the future floating around. What is the city theater of the future? Yuvviki, as somebody who's worked at one of these city theaters of the future, can you tell us what needs to be the city theater of the future?*

DIOH I'm precisely this type of institutional representative who really tries to think about tokenizing, about democratization without fetishization. I try to be a beacon of hope because with this current artistic direction, these were exactly the questions we tried to implement and find institutional answers to. How do we create rooms? How do we create moments where people meet and talk to each other? It's about transmitting knowledge. Switzerland—similar to what Noah Lena said about Belgium—is fragmented between the four different languages. Because of the hegemony of German playwrights, we've pushed for more Swiss German pieces. I think a city theater of the future needs to critically observe and analyze how we implement and institutionalize critical social justice practices within productions. A city theater of the future really needs to focus on transformation processes but must acknowledge that it's a political institution. Nothing irritates me more than when people act like theater is an apolitical institution. There must be an understanding that it's deeply embedded in society and political structures, with many political debates mirrored onstage and offstage. I think a city theater of the future really needs to take its time to figure out what we are here for, what we are doing, and why we are doing it. It's like Kopano said, institutions just want to exist in perpetuity. Okay—but why? What is the purpose? What do we really want to give? How do we want to be part of the city? And do we want to be a place where people can actually go to and learn?

For me, theaters are really institutions of learning, an alternative to academia, which has such a high price. The theater can be more accessible as spaces of learning and can also be experienced beyond language and text, with aesthetics, with things you feel and experience. Let's stop for a moment and realize how important we are, especially when we see all these right-wingers coming in. I mean, Switzerland is not in the EU, but we definitely have the same things happening. Especially in a German-speaking traditional municipal theater, where there is a dominance of spoken language, you have this realism that is often translated into humanism and universalism. What I've observed is how through opening aesthetics and forms of narration, you also open up to more diverse people. So it's diversity in creation and diversity in creators as well. The last thing I'm going to say, which I think is really important for a city theater of the future, is to really tap into the potential of dramaturgy when it comes to questions of transformation, be it institutional dramaturgy or the job in itself, because it is a function of critical reflection, education. It is really the key when we talk about transformation, when we talk about antiracist and antidiscrimina-

tory work. I think there is such huge potential when we widen dramaturgy—institutional and production—because dramaturgs, for example, are the ones who need to work with all relevant players of a production: technicians, the ensemble, the artistic direction, while also dealing with finances (sometimes). The municipal theater of the future really needs to tap into this potential.

CLIMENHAGA *That's really beautifully put. Just to finish, I'm going to ask everyone for three words to describe your city theater of the future.*

VERCAUTEREN I think *community*, *development*, and *learning*.

ARISTIZÁBAL I would say *encounter*, *practices*, and *cocuration*.

BLAUE Making art without (financial) purposes. That's four (or five).

VOLKLAND Like a garden. Not in perfection. In constant changes.

MOUAK *Disagreements*, *creation*, and *forward*.

KORTE *Utopia*, *community*, and *challenging*.

MAROGA *Mycelial. Critical. Generous.*

DIOH I think it's *complexity. Critical.* And *loving.*

Marta Keil

What Can We Learn from Tired Institutional Bodies?

Some Speculative Exercises for Times of Exhaustion

The body is tired.[1]

It looks solid, though—standing firmly on the ground, well rooted, well equipped.

It moves gently while breathing, but otherwise remains rather static. It actually barely leaves its place. Its every move is slow: a faster pace would damage the majesty and risk shaking its foundations. They need to remain solid and they need to remain seen as such.

The body is quite noisy at the same time. It speaks, constantly speaks, sometimes roars, sometimes yawns, swallowing up those who happened to be nearby and did not notice what was coming.

Its shape is far from humanlike, but it can warmly hug, greet, protect, nourish, care for, exploit, abandon, and break someone's heart—as human bodies do.

When you look closer, you realize how porous its skin is, but because porosity is often seen as a weakness, the body is covered with extra layers of materials of various kinds. They protect it, hold it together, insulate it.

An institutional body, anxiously guarding well-known modes of working; exposed to a political or economic danger; meticulously exploiting all the human and other than human resources it has access to, it struggles to understand how to stop exhausting everyone around—including itself.

Stretched to its limits, it frantically tries to maintain its balance between the conflicting needs to always take a stand, to remain highly competitive while filling budget gaps, to respond to the political urgencies, to follow the logic of ceaseless growth while creating a critical discourse about it, to claim what "good art" is, to dare to experiment, to prove its efficiency, to win more audience, to boldly set new trends, to defend new trends.

It is tired, too tired to think it could not be.

Pause as Resistance, Tanzfabrik Berlin, Berlin, Germany, 2022. Photo: Anna Stein

Theater 55:2 DOI 10.1215/01610775-11683520
© 2025 by Marta Keil

Thinking Bodies

Following the speculative proposal of understanding "festivals as thinking entities," articulated in the conversation between Daniel Blanga Gubbay, Judith Blankenberg, Silvia Bottiroli, Livia Andrea Piazza, and Berno Odo Polzer, I find it useful to imagine performing arts institutions (including festivals) as thinking bodies.[2] The idea is not to anthropomorphize art institutions or visualize them as human beings but to offer an imaginative framework that can prove very helpful in analyzing their social situatedness and political potential, and in better understanding what actually happens when they get exhausted.

While the wave of chronic fatigue and burnout seems to be rising in the European performing arts, it is increasingly spoken of publicly not as a personal failure but as a social condition, resulting from decades of operating under the pressure of late capitalist, extractivist principles.[3] Many of us art workers are tired, and many art institutions also seem to be. What if we looked at performing arts institutions not simply as entities and (infra)structures only but as actual living bodies that need nourishment and rest and that are often too good at neglecting these needs? What actually steers the physiology and vitality of a performing arts institution? How does it nourish its collaborators and companions, and what kind of nourishment does it, in turn, need? What responsibilities and possible political agency does an institutional body entail?

Pause as Resistance.
Photo: Nara Virgens

Let's imagine the institutional body has its physiology, its rhythm of operating, a structure that keeps it together, and various surfaces that enable it to interact with the other bodies and ecosystems. The institutional body, deeply embedded in a local and transnational context, constantly resonates within it, being closely entangled with human and nonhuman companions, actively shaping its direct and broader surroundings and, at the same time, depending on them (no matter how much effort they put to protect itself from that dependence or to ignore it at all costs). Thus, the institutional bodies consist of their infrastructure, human and nonhuman actors, and the ecosystems they are situated in—and, crucially, the constantly transforming relations and intra-actions between these elements.[4]

From this perspective, based on relational ontology, the shape of a theater institution is never set in stone: it's not a fixed entity, run by some abstract laws that are impossible to change—which paradoxically is a social imaginary that many institutions try to defend. The institutional body is thus not a singular being, a machine, but an ever-changing constellation of human and nonhuman beings (including the local ecosystem, landscape, neighboring community, society; local and international art scene, etc.); a collective body that is possible only thanks to the ones who at the moment coshape it, and that, at the same time, differs from them, becoming something else than just a sum of many other bodies and entities. This constellation is temporary: it becomes possible only in the moment when all its elements meet and because of how they meet—before changing again, following another artistic practice, other publics, and so on. Because of these changes, the way the institutional body breathes, perceives, and experiences also transforms.

It is through these intrarelations that the institutional body breathes, touches, gets nourished, and nourishes others. In that sense, an institutional body is a living body, as it transforms constantly, and in nourishing its environment(s), it also gets its own needs nourished. If the main responsibility of the art institution is to create conditions for artistic practices to develop and build relations with their audiences, then understanding the rhythm of its body is crucial to secure the continuity of resources that it needs to operate. This is precisely why this speculative exercise could be interesting for institutional critique: hopefully it might help us to understand that if an institutional body continues to follow the late capitalist logic of ever-deepening alienation, without allowing itself getting regenerated and nourished through rest and relations, it will inevitably stop being able to do what it was created for.

DRAMATURGY OF EXHAUSTION

What actually happens when this institutional body gets tired? Dramaturgy of the institutional body's exhaustion is that of disruption, abandonment, loss, and (slow) disappearance. And, often, a heartbreak.

First, its operational time is being hijacked: a flow of production is disrupted, the modes of operating get slower—yet not bringing rest in turn. It's not that the institution stops being efficient; rather, it stops understanding what this efficiency is for. The exhausted institutional body might not show symptoms for a long time, however. It often continues pushing for efficiency and putting all the effort in pretending that everything works fine. It seems it has no choice: the extractivist logic of late capitalism, which dominates production systems in the arts, is the based on ceaseless competition, permanent pressure to produce new and always more attractive ideas, lack of stability, and ever-deepening alienation of art workers and art institutions. There is no space for a break or withdrawal, and if one dares to attempt a break or withdrawal, it risks disappearing out of artists', audiences', and funders' radar. Once you do not produce, you're not seen anymore.

While operating under this constant pressure, the bodies of art institutions and the bodies of art workers often remain malnourished and drained, especially while inhabiting the independent field.[5] Yet we barely meet in this exhaustion. The institutional bodies are often frantically busy protecting their imaginary of being stable, solid, and resistant to change. The precarious bodies of art workers often are too tired to move yet another institutional wall again.

Clearly, operating constantly in the fight mode is not possible. Once the resources are exhausted, the flight mode kicks in: the institutional bodies ultimately become too tired to even think another way is possible. This is when the slow disappearance starts. The principles that the institution has been driven by fade in confrontation with urgent attempts to keep the body afloat; the courage to experiment is replaced by the need to protect oneself at all cost; the rhythm of relational exchange is disrupted, replaced by a permanent crisis and an ever-deepening alienation; team members leave, and the ones who stay anxiously try to protect their own relevance.

The widening gap between the program concept and the practice is particularly painful: the desire to create a fairer, more just organization is often thwarted by the need to adhere to a deeply extractivist logic of production in order to keep going. This is exactly the disruption that makes it impossible to continue in a long run—it will inevitably lead to cynicism or burnout.[6] Passion will eventually die out, trust will disappear, nutritional resources will be depleted.

And then another team comes in. How can they avoid entering the same trap? How can they hold space for their institutional body to regenerate?

Dramaturgy of Withdrawal and Dramaturgy of Rest

This was exactly the moment, shortly after changes in the management team, when Tanzfabrik Bühne, a Berlin-based production house focusing on contemporary dance, choreography, and performance, decided to cease their activities and launch a month-long institutional pause. Let's take a look at this example of a performing arts institution that decided to temporarily disrupt its working rhythm before it would be too late, before yet another crisis would consume all their energy and resources.

Pause as Resistance.
Photo: Nara Virgens

Tanzfabrik is an independent organization, publicly funded by the city of Berlin and active in international collaboration projects supported by European Union (e.g., apap network). It has two branches that operate autonomously, each with its own leadership teams: Tanzfabrik Schule, based in Kreuzberg, which focuses on education, and Tanzfabrik Bühne, situated in Uferstudios in Wedding, which is a production house.

In May 2022, when Tanzfabrik Bühne decided to go for a pause, its institutional body seemed very tired.[7] What certainly contributed to this fatigue was the two-year-long crisis management related to COVID-19 pandemic (lockdowns, cancellations, opening anew, adapting to new restrictions, further lockdowns). Another important factor was a stressful moment of transition in the artistic leadership: this type of change, however essential, can be particularly demanding for an institutional body. The process of acknowledging that the previous modes of working did not sustain, saying goodbye to old patterns and people who shaped them, and then welcoming new ones who might have a lot of ideas and genuine passion to make them real but still need to find their own ways of doing that—this transformation is always risky, as it disrupts the institutional rhythm. And even if it was certainly not the first time the institutional body of Tanzfabrik Bühne got tired, this time the symptoms seemed impossible to ignore any longer.

In the announcement text *Pause as Resistance*, Lanteri and Zeedan wrote,

> We understand pausing as a subversive act of refusing the non-essential and mak-
> ing space for what matters most: reflecting, regrouping and taking time to initiate
> changes. Both in our organization and our surroundings. Time to ask ourselves:
> How do we do things? Which material conditions do our activities take place in?
> What are we automatically reproducing? How we can be a feminist organization?
>
> Pausing is a decision to refuse to perpetuate this constant actionism, constant
> production, and to not accept that there is no way out of capitalism. But to resist it
> and maybe find a place on its margins, from where we can start a revolution.[8]

For a month the institutional body of Tanzfabrik Bühne was put to rest. The everyday
activities were suspended: no performances took place, no rehearsals were conducted,
no meetings taken or calls answered.[9] That does not mean, however, that Tanzfabrik
held its breath for a month: the refusal to carry on as usual did not exactly mean doing
nothing. Instead, the institutional body of Tanzfabrik was experimenting with taking
its breath at another, slower pace and in a companionship with another constellation of
other bodies (artists, audiences, books read during that month, the infrastructure and
landscape of Uferstudios).

The team has not abandoned the venue: they were invited to still come every day
to work and to take a moment for collective reflection and rest. In addition, Tanzfabrik team invited four artists to join the month of pause: two international ones, invited
by the apap Feminist Futures network (Florin Flueras and Harun Morrison), and two
based in Berlin who answered an open call and were selected through a lottery (Ana
Libório and Dafne Narvaez). Once a week, the collective rest was open to the public,
which was invited to come to Uferstudios and join the pause.

For some time, the team and artists spent all this time together in one of the stu-
dios, reflecting their work and principles, participating in somatic practices, reading
and gradually creating a common library, doing all sorts of things that were put on hold
forever because there were always more urgent things to do.

Then some team members who focus on administration and accountancy decided
they needed some time on their own, so they came back to their offices. On the one
hand, it was a perfect proof that not all members of institutional team can afford to
withdraw: some actions still had to be taken (contracts needed to be signed, bills paid).
On the other, for some people, taking rest might mean being able to calmly continue
their work, without the disruption of everyday rush, team meetings, and stress of urgent
questions coming all day long from various directions.

At the end of the day, the rule of not checking emails for the entire month was
not upheld by most of the team members—partly out of fear of missing something
urgent and being overwhelmed by the number of unanswered emails after the pause,
and partly because we are all so well trained to be productive:

At the end of the first week, many of us were already checking our emails again. We told ourselves that we wanted to do so, so as not to be flooded by a torrent of emails when the pause is over. In reality, we were all a little stressed that something might land on our table requiring our immediate attention. We didn't acknowledge this feeling until later on, but it was our brain conditioned so thoroughly to resist the pause as well.[10]

From the perspective of institutional body's rhythm and modes of operating, *Pause as Resistance* consisted of three main shifts: a spatial one, a shift from body that constantly speaks to the one that listens, and a shift in curatorial practice. The first one manifested in emptying not only the stages but also the offices: the team would meet in the studio, a space usually reserved for artistic practice only. The offices, as spaces connotated with the everyday organizational, administrative, and emotional labor, were intentionally abandoned (at least by the majority of the team). The second shift happened when the institutional body turned from speaking to listening. Instead of filling (public) space by curatorial program, the studio space created conditions for listening: for the team to listen to each other; for the artists to speak with the audience otherwise than through a production presented onstage—and to listen to them; for the audience to speak and listen outside the stage framework. And finally, there was a shift in understanding the principles of curatorial practice: the new leading team of Tanzfabrik took a risk to withdraw from well-known paths of curating programs, and experimented with curating conditions for disruption, for not-doing, and for allowing the unknown to happen.

The temporality produced by the gesture of withdrawing is particularly fascinating: a crack in a linear, productive time, a sabotage of efficiency, that "disrupts actuality to show—or at least it assumes—that there is more than a single present, that there is a potentiality not yet tapped into, not yet actualized."[11] This disruption is crucial to be able to think again beyond the horizon of the next deadline.[12] Suspending everyday flow of productivity and efficiency seems essential to break the trap of capitalist realism and to dare to imagine again another way of working. In a sense, this disruption is key to preventing another one: namely, opening a gap between the ideas and the practice so wide that exhaustion or cynicism seem the only possible outcome.[13]

Pause as Resistance.
Photo: Hilla Steinert

In our conversation in 2024, Lanteri and Zeedan pointed out that one of the main reasons to plan a month of pause was their resistance against having another fundamental discussion about the institutional principles rushed between other meetings, emails, reports, and deadlines. The reflection on what the institution under a new artistic leadership really wants to do and how it might be possible felt more urgent—and to take it seriously, creating proper conditions (making time and space) was necessary. *Pause as Resistance* proved that this could be done, but as an exception, as a temporary disruption of the institutional rhythm of hosting, creating, delivering, reporting.

This gesture of going off the trail for a month provoked a risky question: What happens if an institution withdraws for a moment? In a sense, Tanzfabrik did what most of art institutions were so afraid of during lockdowns: it disappeared for a while. It did not vanish entirely, of course: the people were still there, and the building and resources too—but they were redirected into collective rest instead of rehearsing and producing. Still, for a while there was no Tanzfabrik as we knew it; its bodily shape has changed thoroughly, becoming something else, something difficult to recognize. Resonating with the internal and external changes of the artistic ecosystem it operated within, it temporarily transformed from an active, protective, and caring body into the body that lies fallow.

Pause as Resistance.
Photo: Nara Virgens

During this month of pause, the institutional body of Tanzfabrik continued to build relations with its artistic community and audiences, but using another tissue. Instead of curated series of events and offering infrastructure and artistic, administrative, and emotional labor to support particular artistic projects, it created conditions for letting go collectively. While lying down, the Tanzfabrik body was still strong enough to hold space for others to join. At the same time, its skin became softer, less rigid, taking time to attune to its surroundings. Perhaps by allowing itself to become somewhat clumsy and vulnerable, for the first time the institutional body took all the space it needed to stretch and yawn. Its breathing became calmer, steadier. Once you happened to be around, it was no longer possible to ignore the fact that it was actually breathing: you could see exactly how the air was being inhaled. How much of it is needed. How it moves through the skin. Which way and where it travels. How much is exhaled.

The gesture of making institutional rest public was an invitation, an uncanny one, for the art workers and art institution to meet in the exhaustion. Not everyone in the art community welcomed that idea enthusiastically, though. It was perceived by some as a luxury, as a privilege that very few can afford, and as a gesture against the main duty of an institution: being constantly available for the artists.[14] Of course, *Pause as Resistance* was possible thanks to the privileged position of Tanzfabrik, an institution situated in Berlin, in a moment of peace, with, back then, a precarious but relatively stable economic situation and access to public, structural funding.[15] At the same time, it raised a key political question: Can institutions get tired? Does an open art institution mean an institution that is permanently available? How could institutional critique be broadened by acknowledging the labor of people behind the institutional engine? What can we learn from the tired body of an art institution?

Interestingly, *Pause as Resistance* was still framed as a project: it was referred as such by the team members in the reflection text *Resisting the Rest: On Pausing a Cultural Institution*, and it was advertised through posters and website and communicated to the funders as such.[16] A project temporality obviously has its consequences. First, it had to be carefully prepared, like all other institutional projects: all program plans for next season and negotiations had to be finalized before May 2022, all possible emails had to be answered, potential problems predicted and preemptively solved. Second, *Pause as Resistance* understood as another program initiative or a project risks becoming an outstanding, temporary experience that might actually reinforce the status quo.

And although the practice of rest comes back to the Tanzfabrik program from time to time, recently, with the Berlin edition of (Im)mobility Salon #1: Institute of Rest(s) by Alix Eynudi in March 2024, it became clear for the team that putting the whole institutional body for a pause again would not make sense soon. As Jacopo Lanteri and Felicitas Zeedan pointed out, in 2024 such a month of break seems impossible to consider because of the radically changed sociopolitical context in Berlin and internationally: several war fronts opened simultaneously not too far from Berlin, a heated debate over freedom of speech, and radical cuts in financing independent performing arts in Berlin, to name just a few. But perhaps repeating *Pause as Resistance* as a one-off project by just one institution really does not make sense no matter the current context, as it would inevitably become another curatorial project, another exception confirming the rule of overproduction, competition, alienation, and restlessness.

One possible solution instead could be to introduce pausing and rest as a permanent condition of everyday work of the institution: a resting on micro scale, in everyday practice. Another option that would definitely be fascinating to imagine is a collective withdrawal, a collective month of pause: What if all performing arts institutions in a city decided to take a month of break simultaneously, in solidarity? Instead of seeing the shows, the audience would be invited to take some rest together with them. They would still encounter the artists on another basis: not consuming their artwork but thinking together or lying down together for a while. Testing other ways of nourishing each other.

Now have a look at the body of a performing art institution somewhere around you. Perhaps it is a theater you work at, or one you visit regularly; or maybe its building sits four blocks away, but the program never encouraged you to go inside. What condition does its body seem to be in? Touch its muscles and tired joints; feel the warmth when possible; acknowledge the cold, flat institutional skin when needed. How does that skin breathe? How could it become more porous? Where does this body get its nourishment from? Who does it take responsibility for? Perhaps you could find good conditions to rest there. Perhaps one day you could take a rest together.

Notes

1. The starting point for this article was "What Can We Learn from Tired Bodies of the Art Institutions?," a lecture given at the Hangö Teaterträff festival in Hanko, Finland, in June 2024, and the conversation with Alexander Roberts during our work on the text "Art Institutions under the Spell of Exhaustion: Reimagining Instituent Practices," *Performance Research* 29, no. 2 (2024): 28–34.

2. Silvia Bottiroli, "How to Build a Manifesto for the Future of a Festival 'Festivals as Thinking Entities,'" in *Curating Live Arts: Critical Perspectives, Essays, and Conversations on Theory and Practice*, edited by Dena Davida, Marc Pronovost, Véronique Hudon, and Jane Gabriels (New York: Berghahn, 2018), 329–39. See also Mary Douglas, *How Institutions Think* (Syracuse, NY: Syracuse University Press, 1986); Paul O'Neill, Lucy Steeds, and Mick Wilson, *How Institutions Think: Between Contemporary Art and Curatorial Discourse* (Cambridge, MA: MIT Press, 2017.)

3. M. Goedhart, M. Chernysh, and C. Poli, "Burnout in the Dance Industry: Reflection of Preliminary Research," report, Association for Electronic Music, University of Groningen, 2024, https://research.rug.nl/en/publications/burnout-in-the-dance -industry-reflection-of-preliminary-research-; Jacopo Lanteri and Felicitas Zeedan,

"Resisting a Rest: On Pausing a Cultural Institution," Tanzfabrik, Berlin, 2022, https://www.tanzfabrik-berlin.de/en/pause-as-resistance-stimmen-reflektionen-fotos; Barbara Raes, *Radiantly Burning Out and Stacking Stones*, FOAM, September 25, 2014, https://fo.am/blog/2014/09/25/radiantly-burning/; Daria Sobik, "Zmęczone," *Dialog* 2023, no 3; Gosia Wdowik, artistic essay, unpublished, DAS Theatre, Academy of Theatre and Dance, Amsterdam University of the Arts, 2022. See also Franco "Bifo" Berardi, *The Soul at Work: From Alienation to Autonomy* (Cambridge, MA: MIT Press, 2009); Pascal Gielen, *The Murmuring of the Artistic Multitude: Global Art, Politics and Post-Fordism* (Amsterdam: Valiz, 2010); Byung-Chul Han, *The Burnout Society* (Stanford, CA: Stanford University Press, 2015); Bojana Kunst, *Artist at Work: Proximity of Art and Capitalism* (Winchester, UK: Zero Books, 2015); Ana Vujanović and Bojana Cvejić, *Towards a Transindividual Self: A Study in Social Dramaturgy* (Oslo: Oslo National Academy of the Arts, 2022).

4. Karen Barad, *Meeting the Universe Halfway: Quantum Physics and the Entanglement of Matter and Meaning* (Durham, NC: Duke University Press, 2007).

5. We write more about it with Alexander Roberts in "Art Institutions."

6. Raes, *Radiantly Burning Out and Stacking Stones.*

7. Jacopo Lanteri and Felicitas Zeedan in discussion with the author, Berlin, March 2024.

8. "Pause as Resistance," Tanzfabrik, https://www.tanzfabrik-berlin.de/en/pause-as-resistance-742a8eff-eb60-42b7-91da-fa678005d411 (accessed July 9, 2024).

9. If you happened to write an email to the Tanzfabrik during that period, you would receive this automatic reply:

> During the month of May 2022 the team of Tanzfabrik Bühne will practice a pause. By this we mean a radical reduction, or a complete interruption of the everyday activities of Tanzfabrik stage department, at all levels. E-mails/phones/social media are not used, meetings are not held, planning and production stand still. Pausing is a form of resistance towards our normative logic of work and the effects to which it is subjected, such as productivity, efficiency, marketing, audience acquisition or the attention economies. With our pausing, we want to take time to reflect, without the routines of the every day, on the ground values of our work as artistic institution, on why we are doing what we are doing and how we can do it better. // For these reasons we will not read your mail! // If it is urgent, please contact us by other means, e.g. leave a message on our answering machine or pass by Uferstudios in our weekly Session Tuesdays between 2 pm and 5 pm. // If your message can wait, please write us again the beginning of June. (Jacopo Lanteri, email to the author, May 19, 2022)

10. Lanteri and Zeedan, "Resisiting a Rest."

11. Pepita Hesselberth and Joost de Blois, eds., *Politics of Withdrawal: Media, Art, Theory* (New York: Rowman and Littlefield, 2020).

12. Bojana Kunst, "The Project Horizon: On the Temporality of Making," *Maska* 27, nos. 149–50 (2012).

13. Raes, *Radiantly Burning Out and Stacking Stones.*

14. Lanteri and Zeedan, "Resisting a Rest."

15. The context of COVID-19 pandemic additionally supported the idea of a break and suspension, as it forced global arts field to withdraw and pause during lockdowns.

16. Lanteri and Zeedan, "Resisting a Rest."

Nelda Muray Prado,
Carola Rebolledo,
and Carolina Araya's
Almas perdidas, La
Dramática Nacional,
Centro Cultural
Matucana 100,
Santiago, Chile,
2017. Courtesy of La
Dramática Nacional

Nelda Muray Prado

Social Outbreak

Chile and the Theater as a Reflection of Its Own History

Around the spring of 2019, the people of Chile began to protest several social injustices that reached their peak when public transport fares rose by thirty Chilean pesos (CLPs). This series of events led to the so-called Social Outbreak, which, although it did not achieve significant changes, left its mark.

"Chile Woke Up": that was the slogan used throughout the Social Outbreak. The sentence can be read in many different ways, but there was a feeling that could be seen in the streets: a strange mix of rage and happiness. Along with acts of vandalism, there were also songs, dances, and meetings in parks where the topics of the debate were discussed, always accompanied by something to eat or drink. It was a widespread atonement.

The popular street demonstration became the parallel narrative, the real feeling of the citizens, beyond what the news or the press tells us about. Isn't that the role of art? From my perspective: totally. Historically, we learn about the feelings of subjects and peoples through their artistic manifestations. It is an inherent duty, it is in artists' DNA, to put their sensitivity (body and soul) at the service of an environment that permeates, modifies, and cries out to express itself.

With Chile socially shaken, artistic expressions began to take more political directions. The street became the stage for various demonstrations of a scenic, musical, pictorial, and literary nature. We witnessed many performances that brought out all the popular discontent, and issues that were dealt with surreptitiously began to come to light, such as police violence, human rights, and sexual dissidence. The real heroes of the country appeared (such as Gabriela Mistral, Violeta Parra, and others), silent marches, and the iconic sculpture by Marcel Solar of a huge black stray dog called Negro Matapacos (Black Cop Killer), a tribute to a mongrel that accompanied the university students to protests and ran with them. That dog became the symbol of the uprising: a pack of mutts barking at the authorities.

In music, Ana Tijoux, Mon Laferte, Nano Stern, and Alex Anwandter did their

Theater 55:2 DOI 10.1215/01610775-11683533

part by participating in protests or making public statements in favor of the Outbreak. Groups like LASTESIS, Yeguada Latinoamericana, and Memorarte raised their voices against the prevailing machismo, abuse, and harassment, and against the silence of the state in the face of this violent and normalized behavior. The Delight Lab collective was in charge of projecting slogans on a huge building at the epicenter of the protests. Likewise, the programming of the cultural centers had to be modified according to what was happening.

Not all the theaters were lucky. The Cine Arte Alameda, located in the recently named Plaza Dignidad, was completely burned and has not yet been repaired. The so-called Teatro del Puente, because it was at the epicenter of the demonstrations, was functioning as a Red Cross center to care for protesters injured by tear gas, pellets, or blows. Two years later, they held an exhibition around the anniversary of October 18,

Nelda Muray Prado's *Las Piedras*, La Dramática Nacional, Dōjo de Práctica Teatral, Santiago, Chile, 2024. Courtesy of La Dramática Nacional

2019, with photos, banners, and records of everything that happened during that period of demonstration and protest, where the phrases were strongly read: "It wasn't depression, it was capitalism," "Not feeling anger is a privilege," or "It wasn't 30CLP, it was 30 years."

At that time, the Agrupación Artística La Dramática Nacional, a multidisciplinary theater company that I lead together with two actresses, Carola Rebolledo and Carolina Araya, was giving performances in penitentiary centers in Santiago and the Fifth Region. This circulation was thanks to the financing of the Ministry of Culture, Arts, and Heritage, within the framework of the program called "Artistic Visits," whose purpose was to bring pieces of performing arts to places of social vulnerability (hospitals, senior citizen centers, penitentiary centers, etc.). Our proposal, as a company, has always been in the narrative of social history, rescuing national authors forgotten or relegated to the theatrical historiological study. In 2018 we showed a trilogy by the author Antonio Acevedo Hernández that we called "Miners, Peasants and Workers," since his works portray precisely those groups of workers who have been the economic support of the country throughout history: silver mining (from the mid-nineteenth century), wheat farming (and later wine growing) from the nineteenth century to the present day, and the work of industrialization, that is, the city and factory worker.

As a group, we felt a certain political responsibility regarding what was happening, especially given the character we had developed: a resilient company in the face of social issues that drag on for years and that do not allow Chile to advance in equity.

And it was logical: anger was growing, and the political class did nothing to calm the masses; instead a series of mocking phrases emerged from the mouths of ministers, parliamentarians, and authorities. It seemed like they were making fun of the working class: for example, "If you want a lower rate, get up earlier"; "Good news for romantics, the price of flowers has dropped"; "People go to the public medical center, not only to see a doctor but to socialize."

It should be noted that from the institutional side, in our country, the situation of art is not resolved, although there is a ministry. Since the return to democracy, none of the governments in power have been able to resolve fundamental issues. Therefore, Chilean artists, for the most part, live in a state of uncertainty (and anger). In the case of cultural spaces, the operation is more or less the same: a few receive state support, but others must operate privately, financing themselves by cutting entrance fees or competing to receive funds for strengthening or equipment.

Obviously, my writing is aimed at the performing arts, since it is the field where I work, but I would venture to say that with other areas of art, such as music or plastic arts, the panorama is similar.

"The seed that begins in the street."

One of the most significant demonstrations, the starting point of this citizen revolution, was carried out by high school students: "the jump of the turnstiles" in the Santiago subway. The people rose up in general discontent and supported the students. From that moment on, nothing was the same in the country's daily social life.

Nelda Muray Prado, Carola Rebolledo, and Carolina Araya's *Almas perdidas*. Courtesy of La Dramática Nacional

Nelda Muray Prado, Carola Rebolledo, and Carolina Araya's *La canción rota*, La Dramática Nacional, Centro Cultural Matucana 100, Santiago, Chile, 2024. Courtesy of La Dramática Nacional

Along with symbolic actions (or art actions) such as the renaming of Plaza Baquedano to Plaza Dignidad, murals, graffiti, and photographs, a series of street performances arose, the best-known of which was the one presented by the group LasTesis, with a strong feminist message that traveled around the world.

In our case, as a group, we were invited to the Chilean National Theater, Antonio Varas Hall, one of the most important and oldest theater institutions in Chile. Echoing what was happening, this theater, under the direction of Ramón Griffero, reorganized its programming and created a short cycle in November 2019 called "Teatro en Emergencia." At that time we presented our trilogy of popular works, and after each performance a discussion was held between the attendees and the creators, just as was happening in the public squares, where self-convened town halls were generated to discuss the issues that had arisen and that, ideally, would lead to a New Constitution of the Republic (which did not happen).

Similar cases occurred on the national billboard. Among the works presented by the SIDARTE Theater (Actors' Union) at the end of October was *Insolvent and Asbestos*, directed by Andrés Céspedes and starring Cristián Figueroa. The story revolves around a worker who, poisoned by asbestos and without any response to his demands, burns himself in front of the Palacio de La Moneda.

In November, the Matucana 100 Cultural Center—one of the largest cultural centers in the country, which was rescued by Andrés Pérez Araya, one of the most important figures in Chilean Theater, and then taken over under the administration of President Ricardo Lagos—staged *El Golpe, un relato de memoria*, a theatrical adaptation of the verses in tents that Roberto Parra Sandoval wrote in different stages of the Chilean dictatorship, directed by Soledad Cruz and starring Nicolás Pavez. In addition, the same center staged the play *Pacification*, written and directed by Nicolás Cortés, a street theater show that tells the story of the so-called Pacification of Araucanía, which sought to bring people closer to the permanent conflict in Araucanía and the repression that the Mapuche people have experienced during the last hundred years.

At the Finis Terrae Theater (which belongs to the university of the same name), the play *The Appearance of the Bourgeoisie* was installed. Its promotional slogans included "A Play That Anticipated the Social Crisis" and "Because Culture Is More Necessary Than Ever, We Extend the Season!" Written by Luis Barrales and directed by Aliocha de la Sotta, the play is about a middle-class Chilean family that faces the crisis of its own relationships in the midst of political and social effervescence.

Although it is impossible to compare the cultural blackout of the civic-military dictatorship headed by Pinochet with the incipient rebirth of the arts during the return to democracy, the Social Outbreak of 2019 did generate an awakening in the performing arts. Artists and venues had to modify their programming to keep up with social demands. As such, this episode exemplifies all those theories about how art is a mirror of society, both a reflection and the unofficial popular voice: to paraphrase Marx, for example, "Art is a reflection of social reality." Delving deeper into aesthetic and psychological reflections, Władysław Tatarkiewicz says, "Art is a conscious human activity capable of reproducing things, constructing forms, or expressing an experience, if the product of this reproduction, construction, or expression can delight, excite, or produce a shock."

From my point of view, art theorists promote the idea of the human being as a

Nelda Muray Prado, Carola Rebolledo, and Carolina Araya's *Chañarcillo*, La Dramática Nacional, Centro Cultural Matucana 100, Santiago, Chile, 2014. Courtesy of La Dramática Nacional

Nelda Muray Prado, Carola Rebolledo, and Carolina Araya's *La canción rota.* Courtesy of La Dramática Nacional

creator. That is, the condition of being a "human being" (and not a machine) cannot be seen superficially, since experiences, memories, concerns, and the subconscious are somehow captured in the work. In the case of theater, this view is very powerful, since we find ourselves face to face with vulnerable human beings who often cannot raise their voice in the face of what is happening around them or within them, and this confrontation gives life and oxygen to creators and attendees. Theater is the voice of the voiceless—especially social theater, understood as a movement that brings to the stage themes that are not commonly explored in the public arena because they disturb and shake the status quo.

I think it is important to mention that art, in both its dissemination and its teaching, has permanently maintained a division between the Northern Hemisphere and the Southern Hemisphere. Our time at theater schools forced us to understand Shakespeare, Stanislavsky, Ibsen, Williams, the cradles of Greco-Roman civilizations, some contemporary authors, and the Northern Hemisphere in general. In a few cases, we reviewed great authors of our Argentine brothers, such as Roberto Cossa, but rarely did the heritage history of our Native peoples appear—their cultural manifestations, popular religiosity linked to artistic expression, and so on. I think that for that reason, since the return to democracy in 1990 certain names have begun to emerge. To a certain extent it was urgent to start being authors after the cultural blackout, but it was a slow process.

In that sense, the Social Outbreak was a great example of creative sowing. But it was not enough.

Chile has historically perpetuated inequality. Here 1 percent of the richest hold almost 50 percent of the country's total wealth, and there are extreme differences between social classes. These statistics do not exclude the arts: the opportunities for growth or dissemination available to artists and institutions differ in important ways. Geography also complicates the situation, since the capital is in the center of the long country, and there is a constant desire to decentralize cultural actions, but Santiago is still the home of most performing arts teaching institutions and cultural centers.

And as I pointed out above, this "seeding" was not enough, perhaps because cultural policies are needed to channel, support, and institutionally sustain the actions that artists and institutions can carry out. Although the state supports some institutions, many others function on a shoestring, and although there has been investment in infrastructure (e.g., new theaters) in areas farther away from the metropolis, there are no resources to sustain a constant program.

In some institutional theaters, such as the Universidad Católica Theater, symbolic gestures were maintained such as a mural of eyes representing the number of eyes mutilated by police pellets. In the GAM (the Centro Cultural Gabriela Mistral), some murals were maintained. SIDARTE was one of the places where a new programmatic clarity could be observed, creating monthly thematic cycles that broadened the call to a multiplicity of artists: "month of theater school graduates," "month of dissidents," "month of tradition." But except for these actions at the institutional level, few differences were marked before and after the Social Outbreak. In any case, there is one exception that somehow diverged from the natural course of this story: the COVID-19 pandemic, which came to erase all human activity for a long time. After this long and lamentable parenthesis, the memory of the cultural institutions showed its fragility.

In the case of the companies, it was different, since creative freedom has allowed the development of themes that emerged in the Social Outbreak, which had always been there, sideways, and which theater workers have been collecting. In critical social events, creative seeds remain, but bringing them to fruition will certainly be a slow process. Just as there was a modified program in the context of the outbreak, it seems that the seed of social theater is here to stay, and an emerging dramaturgy is rescuing events or characters from the history of Chile to put them on the stage both to pay homage and to remember what we do not want to repeat. With Maestro Gabriel Salazar (winner of the Chilean National History Award), we wrote a historical drama about the life of Luis Emilio Recabarren, which aims to hit the stage soon. The promotion of this book allowed us to see on the ground the popular desire to know more about the history of our Chile. Apparently that is what is coming.

Milo Rau speaks
at the presentation
of the Vienna
Declaration, Wiener
Festwochen, Vienna,
Austria, 2024. Photo:
Inés Baucher

THE VIENNA DECLARATION

Introduced by Milo Rau

Translated by Lily Climenhaga

There's a quote from the Swiss director Jean-Luc Godard that goes, "To make a film means to change the way films have been made." In the context of a theater or festival, it is not enough to make a good festival. It requires an understanding of how, by whom, and for whom an artistic program is made. It is about examining the festival's methods, subjects, and audiences: to open curation, to diversify the program, and to democratize the access to and breadth of the program. Although the conversation in the field of art always concerns transparency, democracy, and collectivity, it is by far the most feudal branch of the public sector.

I wanted to change that—not in the context of debates and program notes but in the deepest legal structure of the festival. It became clear to me that whatever the measures and regulations would look like, we would first need a constitution that was both generally recognized and written as democratically as possible. I wrote the Ghent Manifesto together with a small group of people, and it mainly concerned the production and technical elements of the City Theater of the Future. When I moved from Ghent to Vienna, taking over Europe's largest interdisciplinary art and performance festival, it was clear to me that that this time I really needed to take the time to develop a methodology for the Festival of the Future. That this time, the declaration should deal not only with production but with all areas of the art world.

Working with a think tank, we identified five central thematic fields—ranging from the question of quotas to ethical ones surrounding Cancel Culture and the #MeToo movement, ecology, access, financial issues, democratizing curation, and so on and so forth—and founded a council made up of a hundred people from the city of Vienna as well as local and international experts. These themes were dealt with in a five-week process that engaged dozens of external experts. Finally, using the roughly two thousand statements collected during the hearings, we passed the ten points of the Vienna Declaration. This process took a total of one and a half years and involved several hundred people.

In contrast to the Ghent Manifesto, the Vienna Declaration is both more comprehensive and less concrete: it is an unpoetic, functional text and its practical details

Theater 55:2 DOI 10.1215/01610775-11683546
81

will, over the next four years (the Free Republic of Vienna has just finished the first of the five cycles outlined in its five-year plan), be further developed by working groups and public conferences. We will devote the Free Republic's forthcoming (second) year to, for example, curation (founding an artistic advisory board), the question of cancel culture, and the code of conduct. Political action is concrete: it is about fixed, clear, institutional practice that is agreed on by the board of directors, the city government, and finally by the Council of the Republic.

The Vienna Declaration is the foundation for this, just as a constitution is in every state. We are accountable to it and can align our concrete development through it: Quotas, yes—but which quotas exactly? Openings, yes—but what does that mean for ticket prices? Democratizing curation, yes—but who will sit on the curatorial advisory board, and how will this board be chosen, and by whom? In the end, it will be five years of hard work, but it will ensure that the wheel of change cannot be turned back. It's not as crazy as many people think. What is crazy is that we're the first festival to have a democratic constitution.—*September 2024*

The Vienna Declaration

Why does an arts festival need a constitution? The values, ideas, and rules that are presented here have been part of curatorial debates for years. Today we are issuing the Vienna Declaration in order to make explicit rules out of implicit ones, to turn ideological debates into concrete decisions. Only a transparent framework makes it possible to work together on equal terms. The Vienna Declaration is a decisive step toward estab-

A Council of the Republic meeting, "Solidarity versus Cancel-Culture," Wiener Festwochen, Vienna, Austria, 2024. Photo: Lily Climenhaga

lishing a "festival of the future," based on the cultural policy mandate of the Wiener Festwochen as a transdisciplinary, producing, and international festival.

Two notions recurred throughout the Council of the Republic debates. An institution that aims to open up and change must first recognize that it is part of the problem. Structural exclusion is constantly replicated. On the one hand, a city festival has to address the people of the city, include them, and listen to them. On the other hand, an international festival has to answer to the global nature of art and open up to the artistic and social practices in the world. We need to develop quantifiable parameters to these ends, to be evaluated and adjusted every year.

The Vienna Declaration was drawn up by the Council of the Republic, a board of eighty Viennese citizens. They are people from all districts of the city; they include school students, apprentices and university students, employees and freelancers, people without jobs and retirees, people who have grown up here and people currently seeking asylum, people of all genders and sexes, people with and without disabilities, people with a range of different biographies, migration histories, and paths through life—as firefighters and teachers, as artists, child psychiatrists and publicans, in social services and in law, as doctors and behavioral biologists, activists and after-school teachers.

For five weeks, sixty experts from the fields of the arts, culture, politics, sciences, activism, and civil society explained their positions on the transformation of the Wiener Festwochen to the council. Almost a thousand statements and suggestions were exchanged in ten sessions. What is the art for our age? How can a festival radically transform its sociopolitical goals?

The following declaration provides a direction. From autumn 2024 onward, several council subcommittees will work on concrete measures to be implemented in the festival incrementally during the coming years. Experts and partner organizations from the City of Vienna, Europe, and the entire world will continue to be invited, heard, and involved in the implementation process.—*September 2024*

First: A versatile program needs versatile perspectives. Program design must not be the privilege of a small group of curators. The Free Republic of Vienna will therefore introduce an alternating advisory committee for the program with local and international expert members.

Second: Comprehensive structural change instead of lip service. The Free Republic of Vienna will define binding quotas for invitations, coproductions, and new productions. The global womxn composers platform *Academy Second Modernism* serves as an example.

Third: The festival belongs to the audience—including the audience that has not yet joined. The radical interconnection of program design, publicity measures, and price policies will serve to call all members of society. The *Volksstück/pièce commune*, which

The Council of the Republic presents the Vienna Declaration, Wiener Festwochen, Vienna, Austria, 2024. Photo: Inés Baucher

toured the entire city in cooperation with twenty-three partners, is a first step in this direction.

Fourth: The political handprint is as important as the ecological footprint. The Free Republic of Vienna will develop a sustainable production, presentation, and touring model together with partners from throughout the world. It will provide a stage for the socio-ecological transformation.

Fifth: Change begins inside the institution. Only a team that reflects the entire scope of society can stage a festival that is relevant to the city and the world. The Free Republic of Vienna will aim to depict the whole range of urban societies in its staff structures.

Sixth: Debate instead of backroom diplomacy. The Free Republic of Vienna will develop plain processes and public formats that can be called on in case of controversies and when demands are raised to exclude guests or cancel artistic projects.

Seventh: The stages of this city are for the people who live in the city. We will develop arts projects together with local communities every year. In line with a modernism without borders, we hold that global exchange fosters urban diversity.

Eighth: The Free Republic of Vienna turns theater into a space of debate. In order to negotiate social realities, we need formats that allow for quick and sustainable reactions to current events. The debates triggered by the *Vienna Trials* are a first example of this.

Ninth: We are committed to a respectful working environment and against every form of discrimination and violence—in front of, on and behind the stage. Codes of conduct will be developed and implemented together with expert support.

Tenth: Who finances the Wiener Festwochen, who reaps the profits? The Free Republic of Vienna will reinforce measures for the critical examination of the past and present income and fundraising structures of the Wiener Festwochen GesmbH with regard to social and climate justice.

*Cárcere ou porque
as mulheres viram
búfalos*, Festival de
Curitiba, Teatro da
Reitoria, Curitiba,
Brazil, 2023. Photo:
Lina Sumizono

Marcos Davi Silva Steuernagel

Rehearsals for an Archaeology of the Future

Curating Brazil in the Festival de Curitiba

"Our curatorial work for the Festival de Curitiba began in one Brazil and ended in another." With these words, Daniele Sampaio, Giovana Soar, and Patrick Pessoa opened the curatorial statement of the 2023 Festival de Curitiba.[1] If anything, it was an understatement. When the last edition closed in April 2022, the COVID pandemic had already killed over 650,000 Brazilians, placing the country second only to the United States in total number of deaths, yet ahead in deaths per capita.[2] Jair Bolsonaro's reelection bid raised serious concerns from the international community over the survival of Brazilian democracy.[3] As in the rest of the world, the pandemic had additionally devastating consequences for performing artists, who could no longer work given social distancing requirements. In Brazil, this blow had been amplified by Bolsonaro's attacks against artists, including dissolving the Ministry of Culture in his very first day as president.

By the time the 2023 festival opened, the pandemic was largely in the past, as a record 85 percent of Brazilians had been vaccinated. Bolsonaro had lost his reelection bid to former Workers' Party president Luiz Inácio Lula da Silva, who made an unexpected comeback from prison. On day 1 of his government, Lula presented the most diverse cabinet the country had ever seen, including the Indigenous leader Sônia Guajajara as minister of Indigenous people, Black activist Anielle Franco as minister of racial equality, and Afro-Brazilian singer Margareth Menezes leading the reinstated Ministry of Culture.[4] This was, indeed, a completely different Brazil.

Under the insightful title "Rehearsal for an Archaeology of the Future," Sampaio, Soar, and Pessoa's curatorial statement reflected this new spirit from the onset:

> Every curatorship is a child of its own time, place, political and social context. We
> need to start by saying that our curatorial work for the 2023 Festival de Curitiba

Theater 55:2 DOI 10.1215/01610775-11683559

Quem tem medo de travesti, Festival de Curitiba, Teatro Paiol, Curitiba, Brazil, 2016. Photo: Kelly Knevels

began in one Brazil and ended in another. And as it should be, the result reflects the tensions and crossings these four months of work produced in us. The list of transformations the present moment sets beyond us is immense. And, even though there is much to be done, the Brazils of the past, the present, and the future have always been, and will always be, plural and diverse.[5]

In this essay I investigate how a long-term curatorial project for a major theater festival can be approached as an institutional dramaturgy for a country. The curating of any large festival involves an exercise of metatheatrical dramaturgy that shapes the way its audiences experience performance even before they engage with the theatrical space. As a practice that inhabits the intersections between the public-facing events and the opaque institutional decision-making, curating is both an archeological process of digging up what performance artists are creating today, and an a posteriori production of a future-oriented narrative that organizes the pieces they were effectively able to program. An archaeology of the future.

The Festival de Curitiba presents a particularly productive case study for the kind of long-term and large-scale analysis I am proposing here. Since its first edition in 1992, it has cultivated a reputation for showcasing national premieres, particularly of very popular actors and theater groups. With the introduction of an uncurated Fringe in 1998, modeled after Edinburgh, the festival grew to become the largest performing arts event in Latin America. Unlike with other major Brazilian festivals, founder Leandro Knopfholz has always approached the festival as a commercial enterprise. In addition to the curated showcase, known as the *mostra oficial*, which typically features around thirty productions, an average edition of the festival includes two hundred to three hundred productions in the uncurated Fringe, the comedy track Risorama, the children-focused Guritiba, the culinary festival Gastronomix, and the variety shows Mish Mash! All included, the Festival de Curitiba typically reaches an audience of over two hundred thousand people and employs over fifteen hundred artists over roughly two weeks.[6]

For the 2016 edition, Knopfholz invited Marcio Abreu and Guilherme Weber, two prominent theater artists who began their careers in Curitiba, to take over the curating of the main showcase. In an interview I conducted with them in 2018, Abreu and Weber referred to their curatorial mission as threefold: speaking to the festival's heterogeneous audiences; establishing an active dialogue with the city of Curitiba; and attracting the most interesting and cutting-edge theater artists from across the country and abroad. Abreu and Weber described how, after decades of a successful formula as "a showcase for the country," the interest of theater critics and specialized journalist in the festival gradually declined, leading Knopfholz to invite a new curatorial perspective. "We want to approach the exercise of curating almost as a discourse in and of itself, a dramaturgy," declared Abreu.[7]

The curatorial statements published in the festival programs since 2016 are my main object of analysis here. In their institutional dramaturgy, curatorial statements are by nature utopic and inspirational in how they map out a heterogeneous selection process. Yet, crucially, they are written by the same people engaged in the burdensome tasks of attending hundreds of hours of performance throughout the country and abroad, contacting and negotiating with producers, inviting and refusing, interfacing with those who hold the infrastructural power over budgets, venues, dates, airplane tickets, hotel reservations, unexpected cancellations. Brazil is a country of continental proportions, yet I argue that the scope and the format of the Festival de Curitiba allows for a reflection not only on Brazilian theater but on Brazil itself. Marcio Abreu and Guilherme Weber curated the festival from 2016 to 2020; Daniele Sampaio, Giovana Soar, and Patrick Pessoa took over in 2023. It would be impossible to thoroughly map the hundreds of plays selected over these nine years in such a short essay, and my writing here is marked both by the thrill of sharing the performances I am able to mention and the frustration about the many more that go undisclosed.[8] I focus, instead, on how these five curators produced an institutional dramaturgy for Brazil through the festival from 2016 to 2024.

When Abreu and Weber began their curatorial work, the country was in upheaval. After thirteen years in government, the Workers' Party was grappling with widespread protests and a far-right insurgency. The Speaker of the House had initiated impeachment proceedings against President Dilma Rousseff, while Lula himself became the target of the major Car Wash corruption probe. This climate of political uncertainty framed the statement for the 2016 festival, which Abreu and Weber named "Reverberations / Transversalities / Unfoldings." Compared to future editions, the statement was short, yet it introduced what Abreu and Weber called "a first step" in their experiment: "How can a festival reverberate beyond its specific instance as an event? What can a festival leave for a city? How has theater reflected on the unavoidable issues of our time?"9

The 2016 festival included large crowd-pleasing productions featuring famous TV Globo actors, such as a double bill of Shakespeare's *Macbeth* and *Measure for Measure* with Thiago Lacerda at Teatro Positivo. Yet the "unavoidable issues of our times" could be seen everywhere: in Teatro de Narradores's *Cidade vudu* (*Voudu City*), a multi-genre reflection on Brazil's forceful military presence in the UN MINUSTAH peacekeeping mission in Haiti, and the Haitian immigrants who since then have poured into the country; in *Batucada*, a site-specific performance that placed a pile of nude bodies in the public streets of downtown Curitiba; in *Quem tem medo de travesti?* (*Who's Afraid of Transvestites?*), an "artistic perspective on the trans universe." Weber recalls a specific production, *Why the Horse?*, as pivotal to their understanding of what curating meant for them. In this play, Maria Alice Vergueiro, who had starred in many of the most iconic productions in the history of Brazilian political theater since the 1950s, staged her own funeral. "I called Leandro [Knopfholz] and said, this is the most important theater event in Brazil, we have to have her die in Curitiba."10

Through Vergueiro's staged death, the theater echoed the unraveling of a political project for the country that was effectively dying on the national stage. On April 17, 2016, just a few days after the end of the festival, Brazil's House of Representatives voted to impeach of Dilma Rousseff in a ten-hour abject political spectacle televised to millions of people across the world.11 Vice President Michel Temer immediately took over as interim president and, in his very first day in power, dissolved Brazil's Ministry of Culture. Although later reversed under significant pushback, this gesture clearly signaled the tumultuous relationship the growing far-right would have with Brazilian artists and intellectuals. Donald Trump's election as US president later that year made the global nature of the rise of neofascism even more explicit, a movement that intentionally targeted artists and intellectuals, conspiratorially accused of taking part in an attempt by "leftist globalism" to destroy "Western civilization."

The program for the 2017 festival inaugurated a format that would permeate all future editions. The curatorial statements now featured prominently across two pages (always pages eight and nine of the hundred-twenty-plus-page brochure) and included a play-by-play exposition of how each invited production fitted within the curatorial vision for that year. Instead of being listed alphabetically with all the other productions, as in previous editions, the curated performances were now featured in their own section, visually highlighting the interconnections and larger themes that organized the productions each year. *Interlocutions*, a new series of gatherings, talks, workshops, and roundtables with invited academics, critics, journalists, and artists, expanded the broader themes of the festival beyond the performances themselves. All combined, the curatorial statement, the conceptual mapping of the selected plays, the visual overview of the invited productions, and the Interlocutions added up to an argument for how the festival actively participated in a much broader conversation on the space of theater within an increasingly antagonistic national and global landscape.

For 2017, Abreu and Weber chose the theme "I'm only interested in what is not mine." Inspired by the work of modernist poet Oswald de Andrade, Abreu and Weber defined their curatorial goal as to "create friction with fundamental issues of our time."

Why the Horse?, Festival de Curitiba, Curitiba, Brazil, 2016. Photo: Annelize Tozetto

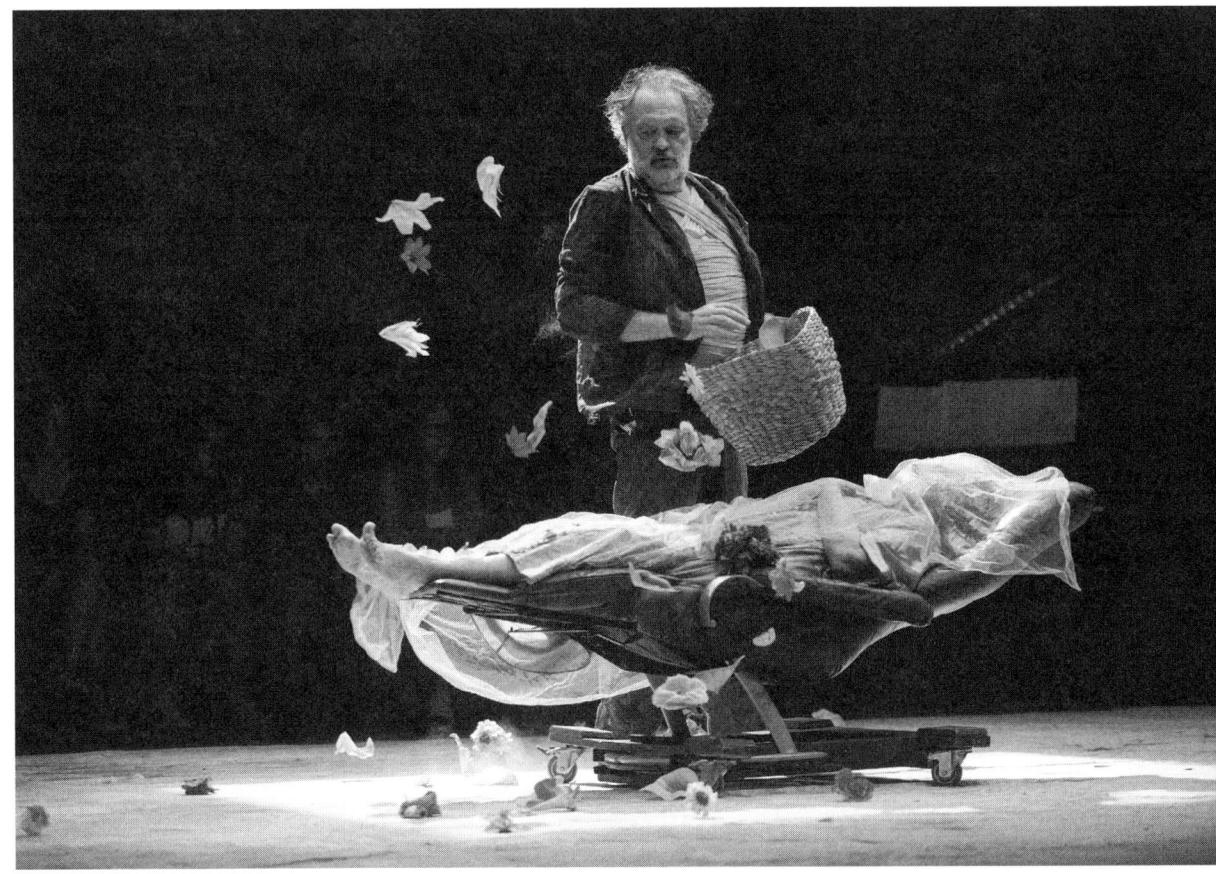

The demise of the Workers' Party in Brazil and the rise of neofascism throughout the world were marked by the increase of openly sexist, racist, and white supremacist tropes in political discourse.[12] Abreu and Weber responded by framing a thread of fifteen pieces they had selected under the header "Women and Identity." These plays included a combative Andrea Beltrão as an Antigone who, in the words of the curators, "painfully recognizes the discourse of the tyrants who ravage our country." Lia Rodrigues, one of the country's most prominent choreographers, was invited to present *Para que o céu não caia* (*For the Sky Not to Fall*), a piece that engaged with Indigenous struggles and the climate emergency inspired by Yanomami Shaman Davi Kopenawa's book *The Falling Sky*.[13] Fernanda Julia's *Macumba: Uma gira sobre poder* (*Macumba: A Gira about Power*) celebrated the "recognition of Black art in a white society that does not recognize it," while Jé Oliveira's *Farinha com açúcar* (*Flour with Sugar*) highlighted "what it means to be the main target of Brazilian police brutality." In the streets of Curitiba, Amir Haddad presented his adaptation of Shakespeare's *The Tempest*, called *Próspero e os Orixás* (*Prospero and the Orishas*), while the collective Toda Deseo from Belo Horizonte

Próspero e os Orixás— a tempestade, Festival de Curitiba, Praça Santos Andrade, Curitiba, Brazil, 2017. Photo: Annelize Tozetto

prominently featured queer and trans bodies in public spaces in *Gaymada* and *Nossa Senhora da (Luz)* (*Our Lady of [Light]*).

In 2018, I was thrilled to be in my hometown of Curitiba for the festival. As a theater student, practitioner, and later teacher, I had diligently attended every festival from 1999 to 2007, when I moved to New York City. Curitiba is a large city of roughly two million people, yet given the festival's compressed timeline and heterogeneous nature, it's hard to emphasize how much it envelops the city. During those two weeks, journalists, critics, and theater practitioners from all over the country move to Curitiba, advertising is everywhere, and even people who seldom go to the theater do so. I had been following the programing from afar, yet I was longing for the embodied experience of once again being immersed in the Festival de Curitiba.

Abreu and Weber chose as the theme for that year the first sentence from the medical report following the homophobic assassination of filmmaker Pier Paolo Pasolini: "If it is of bodies and cities that we must speak."[14] In their statement, they presented Brazil as a country tempted by its desire "to renew its marriage with violence as a way to solve political and ideological conflicts." In an openly pessimistic reading of the country, they argued that the plays for that year were selected "in times of every kind of intolerance." At Teatro José Maria Santos, Márcio Abreu's *Cia.* Brasileira's production of *Preto* (*Black*) presented "racism as part of the mentality of Brazilians." I was at the SESC da Esquina theater for Fernando Kinas's *Manual de autodefesa intelectual* (*Handbook for Intellectual Self-Defense*), a Brechtian forum on contemporary mysticism and obscurantism, when an audience member stood up and loudly protested that she had "paid a ticket to see theater, and not listen to politics."[15] At Grupo Obragem, I listened attentively to Renato Livera's intimate musings on the many meanings of the word *colony* in *Colônia*. At Teatro da Reitoria, I witnessed an enthusiastic standing ovation for *Domínio público* (*Public Domain*), a play the festival coproduced with artists who had been persecuted by the "wave of conservatism and intolerance that devastated Brazil" over the previous years.[16] In the streets of Brazil, a general affect of depression had taken over as we transitioned from the hopeful rhetoric of the Workers' Party toward the emerging neofascist discourse of what we would learn to call Bolsonarismo. Yet inside the theaters, the mood was of celebration of diversity and resistance through the arts.

In the interview I conducted with Abreu and Weber that year, they underscored the significance of curating a theater festival within a context of increased political polarization. "The role of the curator is not to tame the audience," they said. "The role of the curator is to generate improbable encounters."[17] The most improbable encounter was not curated by them. On April 7, one day before the festival ended, the whole country watched 24/7 live coverage of Lula being arrested and imprisoned by order of judge Sérgio Moro. With Lula, the leader in the polls, unable to run, Jair Bolsonaro was elected president of Brazil and appointed Moro as his minister of justice.

For the 2019 festival, Abreu and Weber's curatorial statement, "The Insurrection That Is to Come," was explicit about their goal of multiplying "small spaces of resistance." In the commentary on the plays, Abreu and Weber presented *Quando quebra queima* (*When It Breaks It Burns*), a play devised by high school students who had occupied public schools in protest, as proposing "a new chapter of struggle and resistance of the youth against the attacks on Brazilian democracy and education." They asked, "What does Blackness and being Black mean in our country?" through productions such *Elza*, a musical on singer and Black activist Elza Soares, *Navalha na carne negra* (*Razor in Black Flesh*), a Black adaptation of a classic dictatorship-era play by Plínio Marcos, and Tarina Quelho's *Isto é um Negro?* (*Is This a Black Person?*), a performatic experiment that emerged from reading Angela Davis, Fred Moten, Achille Mbembe, bel hooks, Grada Kilomba, Frantz Fanon, Sueli Carneiro, and Aimé Cesaire.

The last edition Abreu and Weber curated was planned for March 2020. The programs were printed, the advertising went out, and tickets were being sold, but as the date approached, it became clear that the festival would not take place. During the global COVID pandemic, Brazilian artists were confronted not only with the threat of a deadly virus but also with the structural dismantling of the funding for the arts and constant attacks from the growing neofascism. The statement for the last edition of the Festival Abreu and Weber curated, the one that never happened, had been presciently titled "What Can a Body Do?"[18]

After a two-year hiatus, the Festival de Curitiba returned in 2022 for a commemorative thirty-year edition. The official showcase, now renamed Mostra Lúcia Camargo,[19] was programmed directly by directors Leandro Knopfholz and Fabiula Bona Passini.[20] I was once again in Curitiba for the 2023 edition, the first one to return to the prepandemic format. Many of the same topics that defined previous editions were still present: structural racism, gender violence, the questioning of Brazilian identity. The largest production that year, *Prot{AGÔ}nistas—o movimento Negro no picadeiro* (*Prot{AGO}nists—the Black Movement in Circus*), featured a celebration of Blackness in theater, music, and circus. In *Cárcere ou Porque as mulheres viram búfalos* (*Prison or Why Women Turn into Buffaloes*), Cia de Teatro de Heliópolis offered a visually stunning and moving reflection on the massive incarceration of Black people in Brazil. *Karaíba*, a play based on the book by Indigenous author Daniel Munduruku, featured the largest team of Indigenous cast, backstage creators, and technicians ever presented in a theater festival in Brazil. In *Sobrevivente* (*Survivor*), Nena Inoue, one of the most important actors of the local Curitiba theater scene, offered a vulnerable and heartwarming journey through her own Japanese and Indigenous roots.

Though these themes were familiar, the affect in both the festival and the country was quite different. In a 2024 interview I conducted with Soar about their curatorial approach, she addressed this change. Soar mentioned that their curatorship was

the first after a six-year institutional crisis that had been inaugurated by Rousseff's impeachment in 2016:

> For the past two editions, the three of us, as curators, have invested in a general atmosphere of festivity, of celebration, of care. That's the basis for our curating. . . . Because we were massacred over these six years. Everything was very hard. The whole artistic environment, artists, spectators, everyone. We were hampered and chased away. So, as curators, we didn't want to deal with this violence anymore. We chose performances that were welcoming.[21]

The political power of care in difference was made even more explicit in the 2024 edition. Under the overarching concept "Curating as the Art of Dissensus," Sampaio, Soar, and Pessoa included a solid set of performances from the Amazon region, including *ÜHPÜ*, a ritual led by Indigenous Tukano performers Bu'ú Kennedy Ye'pá Mahsã and Txana Bake Huni Kuin, and *TA—Sobre ser Grande* (*TA—About Being Great*), a contemporary dance piece featuring twenty-three ensemble members from the Corpo de Dança do Amazonas. The Festival de Curitiba has a long tradition of showcasing some of its most impressive productions to government officials, festival sponsors, and the audience at large in their opening event. In 2024, the opening featured representa-

Isto é um Negro, Festival de Curitiba, José Maria Santos Theater, Curitiba, Brazil, 2019. Photo: Humberto Araujo

95

Caprichoso e garantido: O duelo da Amazônia, Festival de Curitiba, Teatro Positivo, Curitiba, Brazil, 2024. Photo: Annelize Tozetto

tives from one of the largest open-air celebrations of popular culture in Brazil, the Boi Bumbá of Parintins.

Describing the Festival de Parintins to a foreign audience is a difficult task. Parintins is a city of under a hundred thousand people located on an island in the Amazon River, a full-day trip from Manaus in the large boats that serve as the main mode of transportation in the region. There are several popular culture festivals involving a similar story of the killing of an ox, the *boi*, across the country, yet the Parintins Festival has grown to become the largest of them all. During a long weekend in late June, over 100,000 tourists travel to Parintins to experience a competition in the Bumbódromo, a thirty-five-thousand-person arena built for the three nights, six hours each, of the festival. Floats comparable to the ones seen in the Rio de Janeiro Carnival are paraded alongside massive ensemble choreographies, while a huge band cheers the allegorical *bois* to dance. Although not well-known outside northern Brazil until recently, regionally the Boi de Parintins is of huge importance, splitting cities and families between the red Boi Garantido and the blue Boi Caprichoso.[22]

The coldest state capital in Brazil and with a significant history of European immigration, Curitiba can feel worlds away from the hot and humid rainforests of the North. The curatorial gesture of opening the Festival de Curitiba with the Boi Bumbá of Parintins brought to the stage some of the most relevant tensions in the country today: the regional inequalities, the place for Amazonian culture in the context of the global climate catastrophe, Indigenous representation and identity within Brazilian theater. Considered within the long-term curatorial arch of the Festival de Curitiba, this improbable encounter exemplified the institutional dramaturgy of the curators in their project for a country that, once again, made space for dissensus.

In "The Paradoxes of Political Art," French philosopher Jacques Rancière argues that any connection between art and politics lies in dissensus. "Doing art means displacing art's borders," writes Rancière, "just as doing politics means displacing the borders of what is acknowledged as *the* political."[23] Thus, I follow the direction of Sampaio, Soar, and Pessoa in their latest curatorial statement to imagine what curating as the art of dissensus might mean for a country as large as Brazil over a period as turbulent as these past nine years. The changes in the political landscape have been nothing but dizzying, from the impeachment of Rousseff in 2016, through the rise of neofascism both in Brazil and abroad, the devastating effects of the COVID pandemic, and the return of Lula from prison to the presidency. Throughout these years, journalists, sociologists, political scientists, have been united by a similar question: What is happening in Brazil?

Through their curatorships, Abreu and Weber, and then Sampaio, Soar, and Pessoa, have addressed this question with the institutional tools of the Festival de Curitiba: its history and access to private and public funding; its relationship to artists and consumers, journalists and corporate marketing directors; its place within national and international networks of theater festivals and cultural policymakers. The funding structures, artistic practices, and political apparatuses in Brazil are quite diverse. Through their selection processes, curatorial statements, play descriptions, and associated events, these curators have crafted a metatheatrical narrative that insists on diversity and dissensus as spaces for productive encounters between theater and politics. This is both an institutional dramaturgy that responded to the complicated Brazil of the past nine years and, most importantly, a future-oriented dramaturgy that, in the words of the curators, presented in the Festival de Curitiba "the plurality of a Brazil that is diverse, powerful, and always in movement."[24]

NOTES

1. Sampaio, Soar, and Pessoa draw the concept of "archaeology of the future," which I cite in my own title, from the performance "Arqueologias do Futuro" by Mauricio Lima and Dadado de Freitas, presented at Casa Hoffman that year. Daniele Sampaio, Giovana Soar, and Patrick Pessoa, "Ensaio para uma arqueologia do futuro," in *Guia Oficial 2023*, ed. Festival de Curitiba (Curitiba: Festival de Curitiba, 2023), 8–9. All translations from Portuguese are my own.

2. Ingrid Oliveira, "Brasil chega a 650 mil mortes por Covid-19," CNN *Brasil*, March 2, 2022, https://www.cnnbrasil.com.br/saude/brasil-chega-a-650-mil-mortes-por-covid-19/.

3. Jamil Chade, "ONU soa alerta sobre eleição no Brasil e pede processo 'sem interferência,'" June 13, 2022, https://noticias.uol.com.br/colunas/jamil-chade/2022/06/13/onu-soa-alerta-sobre-eleicoes-no-brasil-e-pede-instituicoes-independentes.htm.

4. João Vitor da Silva Marques, "Profile: Brazil's New Culture Minister Margareth Menezes," *Euronews*, January 9, 2023, https://www.euronews.com/culture/2023/01/09/profile-brazils-new-culture-minister-margareth-menezes.

5. Sampaio, Soar, and Pessoa, "Ensaio para uma arqueologia do futuro."

6. Festival de Curitiba, "Mais que cultura, Festival de Curitiba aproxima pessoas e promove negócios," *G1*, April 17, 2023, https://g1.globo.com/pr/parana/festival-de-teatro-de-curitiba/noticia/2023/04/17/mais-que-cultura-festival-de-curitiba-aproxima-pessoas-e-promove-negocios.ghtml.

7. Marcio Abreu and Guilherme Weber, interview by author, Curitiba, Brazil, March 29, 2018.

8. For an excellent photographic overview of the first thirty years of the festival, see Lenise Pinheiro, *Festival de Teatro de Curitiba* (São Paulo: Edições Sesc, 2024).

9. Marcio Abreu and Guilherme Weber, "Reverberações / Transversalidades / Desdobramentos," in *Guia Oficial 2016*, ed. Festival de Curitiba (Curitiba: Festival de Curitiba, 2016), 7.

10. Abreu and Weber, interview, March 29, 2018.

11. For quotes from the vote, see Jonathan Watts, "Dilma Rousseff: Brazilian Congress Votes to Impeach President," *Guardian*, April 18, 2016, https://www.theguardian.com/world/2016/apr/18/dilma-rousseff-congress-impeach-brazilian-president.

12. For an exhaustive analysis of the changes in political rhetoric over this period, see Idelber Avelar, *Eles em nós: Retórica e antagonismo político no Brasil do século XXI* (Rio de Janeiro: Record, 2021).

13. Davi Kopenawa, *The Falling Sky: Words of a Yanomami Shaman* (Cambridge, MA: Belknap Press of Harvard University Press, 2013).

14. Marcio Abreu and Guilherme Weber, "Se é de corpos e cidades que devemos falar," in *Guia Oficial 2018*, ed. Festival de Curitiba (Curitiba: Festival de Curitiba, 2018), 8–9.

15. Michele Marreira, "Mulher interrompe aos gritos peça no Festival de Curitiba," *Blog do Arcanjo* (blog), March 29, 2018, https://www.blogdoarcanjo.com/2018/03/29/mulher-interrompe-aos-gritos-peca-no-festival-de-curitiba/.

16. I wrote about the experience of being in Curitiba in 2018 and attending *Domínio*

Público in Marcos Steuernagel, "*Domínio Público*: Performing the Brazilian Conservative Turn," *Latin American Theatre Review* 52, no. 2 (2019): 129–47.

17. Abreu and Weber, interview by author, March 29, 2018.

18. Marcio Abreu and Guilherme Weber, "O que pode um corpo?," in *Guia Oficial 2020*, ed. Festival de Curitiba (Curitiba: Festival de Curitiba, 2020), 8–9.

19. Lúcia Camargo was one of the main curators for the Festival de Curitiba in its original format until 2015. After she passed away in 2020, the festival renamed the main showcase after her.

20. Festival de Curitiba, ed., *Guia Oficial 2022* (Curitiba: Festival de Curitiba, 2022).

21. Giovana Soar, interview by author, Curitiba, Brazil, July 12, 2024.

22. For more on the Boi de Parintins, see Diego Omar da Silveira, Elizandra Garcia, and Ericky Nakanome, eds., *Os Bois-Bumbás de Parintins: Novos olhares* (Manaus: Editora UEA; Autografia, 2021); Maria Laura Viveiros de Castro Cavalcanti, *Rivalidade e afeição: Ritual e brincadeira no Bumbá de Parintins* (Manaus: Editora UEA; Autografia, 2022).

23. Jacques Rancière, "The Paradoxes of Political Art," in *Dissensus: On Politics and Aesthetics* (London: Continuum, 2010), 149; emphasis in the original.

24. Daniele Sampaio, Giovana Soar, and Patrick Pessoa, "Curadoria como arte do dissenso," in *Guia Oficial 2024*, ed. Festival de Curitiba (Curitiba: Festival de Curitiba, 2024), 8–9.

Leanna Brodie
and Jovanni Sy's
Salesman in China,
Stratford Festival,
Stratford, Ontario,
2024. Photo:
David Hou

Roundtable

"Care Is What Fills in the Cracks"

A Conversation with Diversity Agents

This conversation has been edited for clarity and concision.

LILY CLIMENHAGA *Hello! We are honored to have you all here from so many different corners of the world. I'm going to first ask you all to please introduce yourselves, as well as what theater you work for, and your role there.*

JUDY VANDEN THOREN I'm Judy. I think I'm the odd one out because I don't work for a theater. I work for the Social Fund of Performing Arts in Belgium. We try to help organizations and art houses become more inclusive and determine where the obstacles for minority groups are.

MŪKONZI MŪSYOKI My name Mūkonzi Mūsyoki. I'm a PhD candidate at the University of Alberta. My research is in Afrocentric dramaturgy, intervention, and interweaving relations. I also work with Old Stories in New Ways, a project in Kenya that works with Indigenous storytelling. Last fall, I joined another project in Uganda, which looks at the preservation of Indigenous cultures and sto-

ries in rural Uganda. I also work with Keith at the Stratford Festival as a new play dramaturg and associate, as part of a program where playwrights are paired with dramaturgs. I'm now working with an African Canadian playwright who is building on Bantu epistemologies, exploring interweaving diasporic and African connections, and commenting on the classic repertoire . . . trying to establish that sense of possibility. I am always speaking in draft, so I leave my comments with an ellipsis . . .

KEITH BARKER My name's Keith Barker. I'm a member of the Métis Nation of Ontario. I'm also a mix of French, English, and Scottish. I come to you right now from Stratford, Ontario, which is the traditional territory of many nations, including the Anishinaabe, Haudenosaunee, Attawandaron peoples, and many diverse First Nations. I am currently the director of new play development at the

Theater 55:2   DOI 10.1215/01610775-11683572
© 2025 by individual authors

Stratford Festival here in Canada, working with artists and playwrights with diverse voices that need special care. I have the wonderful luck of getting to work with people like Mūkonzi, who come in, get to work, and share their knowledge with artists trying to tell stories from their point of view.

YUVVIKI DIOH My name's Yuvviki—Yuvvi—Dioh. I'm from Zurich, where I've been the diversity agent of the Schauspielhaus Zürich for about two and a half years. I'm responsible for the diversity-oriented organizational development of the whole institution on

Vern Thiessen's *The Diviners*, Stratford Festival, Stratford, Ontario, 2024. Photo: David Hou

the levels of program, personnel, and audiences. It's a large and really diverse job in itself, where I work with a lot of artists on both production and programming. I work with the ensemble, I visit rehearsals and talk through questions of representation, of people either reproducing problematic things or trying to go deeper into the questions of who is telling whose story, why, and to what effect. We do a lot of community outreach and community building to reach those communities historically excluded from the institution and Zurich's marginalized communities. We try

to work locally, but it is an international institution, as is the city itself.

MAIRI BRASCOUPÉ I am Mairi Brascoupé. I am Algonquin from Kitigan Zibi, I live in Ottawa on Unceded Algonquin territory, and I work for Indigenous Theater at the National Arts Center (NAC). I've been working there for almost seven years now. I'm the cultural advocate for the Indigenous theater, which is a pretty vague title. I do a combination of things. A lot of it is community and education programming, but the goal of my work is to create a more welcoming space for both Indigenous artists and audiences in a very colonial institution: public programming, internal programming, policymaking, all sorts of fun stuff. The Indigenous theater just had our fifth anniversary, but the NAC is over fifty years old. This means we've had to change a lot of things and we're slowly changing them to make it a better place for both our audiences and our artists.

NOAH LENA VERCAUTEREN *Just to start our discussion, what do the concepts of diversity and inclusion in theater mean for you?*

VANDEN THOREN Those are a bit of container terms. Everybody uses them and they put everything into them. But I think for me, if you work around diversity and inclusion, you have to talk about power dynamics and redistributing power because—at least in Flanders—power is very concentrated, not only formal, official power but also informal power. These power dynamics make it a very closed environment and very difficult to be really inclusive. So, for me, diversity and inclusion means making the power dynamics transparent and visible, and then breaking it open and redistributing power.

MŪSYOKI Just to add on to that: What is institutional culture about, and how does it approach the idea of diversity as enrichment and not something additional? Part of it is to wrestle with the politics of inclusion and who is invited into the space. Is it a long-term commitment? What does sustainable intervention mean? For me, cross-cultural explorations come with friction, but also hesitation, because initially that work is not seen as profitable—at least not in how it's framed. It's interesting to look at it in terms of what will happen in the long term, because the short-term outcome is the relations you build. Relations are the central unit, especially sustainable ones. I always find myself tussling with the question: If you approach the work, are you making an invitation that is only temporary? What does that mean? There is also the friction of having to wrestle with the idea of making the people you associate with and their contribution feel valuable. This means being able to partner with the history of performance culture, as well as looking at and challenging its colonial legacy and looking outside the frame. I think part of it is a question of imagination.

DIOH It's really important to tell people that this is deeply political work. Working towards antidiscrimination, towards social justice, towards everything; these right-wingers want to try and tell us that we're woke. Yeah . . . it's woke work! You have to do it! I feel like a lot of times, like Judy said, diversity and inclusion is a terminology that's big and broad and being used a lot. I find myself fighting these very corporate usages of the concept and the terminology. It's about these relations that Mūkonzi talked about. We have to take care of them in all directions and build them sustainably. This in itself is a political feat, political work. In the Schauspielhaus, we want to be a space where different realities and different experiences can meet in a very positive and nourishing space. Why do we do theater? To think about being human, about what our society is, about conflicts . . . to pro-

duce knowledge differently than, for example, academia, which has more strict criteria for producing knowledge, or different criteria than theater. We recognize differences and we show the differences; we try to go beyond just talking about diversity. We think about the power dynamics between groups. We think about histories. We think about the distribution of resources. We think about how we create. Ultimately, it's about creating a space that belongs to everybody. Right?

BRASCOUPÉ Echoing everybody else, it's first acknowledging what powers are there, what audiences or artists are being served in our institutions, and acknowledging how limited that is most of the time, then looking at the diversity in our communities and seeing if the work is actually reflecting or serving that. But until that acknowledgment is there, it's quite a battle. This means acknowledging that we still largely present work by middle-aged white men for middle-aged audiences, or Indigenous work for largely non-Indigenous audiences. Are we fetishizing our work? It goes beyond presenting diverse artists to presenting work for diverse audiences. What does that mean? Is that accessibility? Is that content? Do these institutions have diverse employees? If all the employees are non-Indigenous, non–people of color, how does that frame the work? Moving beyond just presenting diverse work, we need to embody diversity in all aspects of the work, not just what's onstage.

BARKER The Stratford Festival is a primarily white institution with a long history. It's important to recognize that even people coming into our lobby have a history with the institution: that they didn't feel safe, didn't feel it was their story, or never felt it was for them. We have three shows this year running simultaneously that engage three different communities: *Salesman in China*, with a primarily international and Asian Canadian cast

Trajal Harrell's *Maggie the Cat*, Schauspielhaus Zürich, Zurich, Switzerland, 2024. Photo: Orpheas Emirzas

and crew; *Get That Hope*, primarily Caribbean Canadian; and *The Diviners*, a Métis story. Each of those shows has different needs: in the room, outside the room, and with our audiences. We ask, "What is a safe space for people who come to the show? What is the safe space for people in the show? How do they come to us?" On the first day, we have a thing called prerehearsal orientation: a landing space. An elder once told me, "Your body arrives in the room, but then your spirit arrives." What does it mean to show up somewhere?

We work through a value system and practice in service of everyone, dealing with conflicts through the lens of courage, generosity, tolerance, patience, humility, and wisdom. Someone once said to me, "You can't be generous or tolerant if you're not patient," and the first thing we do is patience. When we start talking about inclusion, it's a living document, because it's always going to be different. It's going to be different people, different shows, different ways in which we work. It's not about finding ten rules. It's about what this room needs in this moment to address ideas about how people feel safe, and how people can work

together on this particular play, because each one of those plays want to speak about different things, and they all mean something to different people. So how do we all come together to tell this story and support each other in telling it together?

I often talk about how we bring everyone into the circle. When we enter a room, I can't just say that we're doing a Métis story and throw them together in a room, then as an institution back away and say, "Okay, go ahead! Go for it!" As an institution, we have to lean in and be present, because you don't just put a group of people together . . . because within that Métis group, there are lots of different dynamics and fraught conversations to be had. Our responsibility is to be present in that room, to witness and learn. Continuous engagement from the institution is the hardest part. It means you have to re-up and say, "Yeah, we're back in and we have to be present all the time." I think we're in a space now, at least I'm finding within the theater community, where there is a fatigue. I think that's the moment we need to step back into the circle and be witness again.

CLIMENHAGA *Something of a throughline is the relationship of you and your individual unique positions to mechanisms of power; not just the power outside the theater but also the way that these institutions themselves are mechanisms, are inflexible, and are oftentimes extremely resistant to Indigenous and non-Western forms—not just theater forms, but forms of creation, forms of coming together. How, within each of your positions and despite the possible risk, do you have to speak back to this power?*

VANDEN THOREN I'm an external facilitator, which gives me a bit more freedom. When we start a trajectory, we start off by saying that this is going to be difficult, this is going to be awkward, you're going to feel discomfort. That's part of the process. Then it's up to you to decide whether you want to sit in that discomfort and learn, or not accept the discomfort and get out. But you have to own that you are not yet ready for a trajectory towards being a more inclusive place. It helps. It's kind of a disclaimer which makes it more comfortable to deal with difficult conversations.

MŪSYOKI For me, the work takes longer to really be infused. Part of it is, What does it mean to initiate that conversation? This sometimes means acknowledging failures and embracing the discomfort of addressing it through reflection and reorganization. It's how we come into collaboration, use our expertise, and acknowledge different levels of experience, because everyone enters the room coming from the need to serve the work. In your question about the risk, it's integral to assess how you define risk within in-process projects. Echoing Mairi, there are still things that need to be negotiated through trust, and intention is always critical. Trust is something that takes time. Even in that first contact, the word that comes to mind is an encounter. It's an encounter. The language is tricky but integral, and

going to what Keith said about values, values also frame what you believe in. If you don't have a diverse staff at the core, then people from diverse backgrounds will take extra weight, and negotiating the possibilities here is tricky. Dramaturgy is about weaving possibilities and opening avenues of intervention.

BARKER I worked at Native Earth, Canada's oldest professional Indigenous theater, a small indie organization. When you work primarily with Indigenous artists, it's very easy to look at those larger institutions and call them out. Now to be embedded within one, suddenly these people are your colleagues. Having to speak with them about some of the institution's problematic natures becomes more difficult but also more necessary. There's a lot of learning in that. My friend Thomas Morgan Jones, who's a playwright and director, always says to his rooms, "We move at the speed of trust." We come into these rooms where people have experienced this kind of work, and it's not gone well, and the facilitator maybe didn't have the skillset to help that room or came in hot on something. Then other people, who have had wonderful experiences, come really openhearted into these spaces, ready to go. How do we have and facilitate these conversations? Often I have to move at the speed of the person with the least amount of trust.

David Abel, an administrator, once said to me, "You've got to spend your goodwill capital early." I always try to remember that. We all have a bank full of goodwill. When we start projects, everyone is very positive. As things go on, we're constantly withdrawing from that bank. If you try to address those things too far down the line, banks are empty, and you go into the negative, and people are upset. Whereas if you actually have the really hard conversation right off the top, try to address it as early as possible, then you have time to gain back their trust and goodwill. I always try to remember that, but it's difficult. I win and lose people all the time. Sometimes I go back to my office and go, What have I done? Why do I do this? Then I realize, I have to be comfortable in that uncomfortable conversation. That has to happen; the only thing I can control is intention.

DIOH This was precisely my experience when I started. I thought, "I'm going to be the diversity agent! I'm going to change this house!" I had this big energy, but I realized early on that I'm pretty close to the source of power. I'm part of the artistic direction, also at the top of the hierarchy. How do I deal with the power I've been given? The last two artistic directors really sat with me and tried to figure out strategies and to learn and unlearn. I even did these workshops with them. They still made mistakes. They're still human. But it made it way easier for me to move about the institution and look at the power dynamics and understand, it's not just these two people in power doing whatever they want, even if it might seem like that. There are other, conflicting sources of power in the institution. The decisions you think are made by one person are actually influenced by a lot of other factors and people. This isn't to excuse them; it's to understand how decisions are made. In that sense, I seldom had to talk back to power. It's more a conversation and negotiation process, and the conversation has to be uncomfortable. But because we work together well, it can be difficult to be completely honest. Not because I care about upsetting people in privileged positions and situations but because I want something to work.

I really like "We move at the speed of trust." When I started this job, I thought we had to act, no nonsense, no excessive talk about feelings or sensitivities. I had to earn trust and learn, especially in theater, feelings or emotions actually matter. You have to fac-

tor them in. We had this very eventful change of artistic directors. I started with two artistic directors who spearheaded this whole transformation and diversity topic, and we faced brutal hate, had a media campaign against us—against me—from right-wing and other media. Eventually it was clear that this artistic direction couldn't continue or wasn't going to be able to continue. They kind of got kicked out for being woke. We now have an interim artistic director who does, let's say, more traditional theater. This was really interesting because, besides all the other problems, he was very keen on this idea of trust. It was like this simplistic Eurocentric humanist perspective, where if we don't talk to each other, we will have racism. He was very upset. He said, "Why don't you people trust me?" And I said, "Why do you just expect us to trust you?" He's in a very privileged position, and I feel like he was very used to people just giving him the benefit of the doubt from the start. I had to explain to him that people like me, people from marginalized communities, we don't get the benefit of the doubt. We had a long discussion about how he just wants to be trusted. Eventually I said, "Well, you have to show us why. We've trusted so many people in these institutions and we've been hurt many times. You need to expand your horizon on this issue." I agreed with him, though, that we can work better if we trust each other. And the trust process is definitely growing.

BRASCOUPÉ We were also very warmly welcomed by our institution when we started. They didn't have to create an Indigenous department; that was their choice. But when we wanted to do things differently, people were surprised. I think they didn't consider that it would be Indigenous and not just a replica of the French and English theater departments. We wanted to do different types of programming, spend our money differently, change our ticketing. We came in with the mindset that we were a brand-new department and can do things differently. To get things done, we had to compromise and work within the existing system, which sometimes went against how we wanted to work. But as we've continued, we've started bringing more of what we actually wanted and how we wanted to work. Trust in the powers-that-be has grown over time. I think we have a lot of space to be critical of the systems we work within, but it is a much slower process than we initially anticipated, because it just doesn't stop. We have shows all the time and people need to get the work done, so it's hard to reflect and change those systems. It moves a lot slower than we hope in all areas. But, having seen the changes within our department, people are more on board and it starts to ripple into other areas of the institution. I

think there's still a long way to go, and people are sometimes still skeptical, but that trust is now there for the most part now that they've seen the results. Hopefully that exists beyond doing stuff with an Indigenous lens. I think changing the way colonial institutions function benefits everybody—not just the people working here, our audiences as well. Hopefully we'll keep going that way.

VERCAUTEREN *I want to build on this idea of necessary actions. We've talked a lot about discomfort, friction, risk, and how uncomfortable and necessary it can be within the process of instituting diversity. How do you facilitate practices of care for the people you are working with, and practices of care for yourself?*

BRASCOUPÉ I think acknowledging that this work includes additional labor and emotional

Mathieu Charles's *Maggot Brain II: A Soliloquy of Ghosts*, MOMO Festival, Rotterdam, Netherlands, 2023. Photo: Salih Kilic

labor, which institutions don't necessarily recognize. That's the first step. I think it helps not being the only advocate, because when you are the sole critical person, it can be very difficult. I'm very thankful that I have a supportive team that centers us as people over employees and that we have people outside our department doing this work as well. We have an audience engagement department that now works more with diversity. We've just hired our second director of diversity and inclusion, so we have another person advocating for our concerns at the senior management level. We put a clause in our artists' contracts for cultural accommodations. It acts like a cultural rider, so if folks need certain cultural-related things, we will accommodate.

When we first started, there were very strict areas in which our artists could smudge, which was a highly debated topic, because they wouldn't let our artists smudge in the dressing rooms. That's the main area they would want to smudge. It took a lot of work with operations to make that possible. It's about honoring the artists' requests and making sure they feel like they're cared for by this institution where they may not have felt cared for or included in the past. Now other departments want to integrate diversity and work with the communities that we're working with. But we don't know if they're going to have the same level of care, so we don't really want to hand off these relationships. That's our next step: making sure these relationships are cared for consistently across the institution. Right now, that's not totally the case, but we're trying. We're also making sure that we're taking time for ourselves. We've started instituting shorter rehearsal periods and shorter rehearsal days. So we've gone from ten- or twelve- to eight-hour days, not just for artists but for our tech crew as well. We're trying to center people as people and then looking at what that means for the work.

MŪSYOKI I always speak in metaphors: I look at care as an ingredient that is put into every stage of the meal for it to be delicious, for the meal to be palatable in a way that it holds everyone. It's foundational, which means emphasizing the codification of care and incorporating care into the conversation so it's not just an extra to the work. It brings an ethics. Keith and I build upon what was established by an antiracism committee—a group of artists appointed by the festival tasked with creating institutional reform and recommending new directions—ensuring their recommendations and accommodations are sustainable, healthy, and foster a healthy work environment. We collaborated on a process called Pathways to Cultural Belonging. It's a living document where, when projects are selected for production, a group of us read the scripts and look at it from a dramaturgical perspective as well as the perspective of artistic creation, ensuring that there's care. It reframes the notion of cultural consultancy, not just as an additional element but as an awareness that cuts across the project, from beginning to realization. It is also present in establishing relationships with new audiences.

Being ready to do work you've not done before entails a lot of negotiation. Support and care is always . . . I can't find the words . . . it's balancing. It's about approaching the work in terms of dispensation of care. It's not just one person making the accommodations, it's an exchange and the potential to learn. When we think about the spirit of collaboration and how we engage with outside expertise, care is something that infuses shows with potential. It is part of the inspiration behind the work. Integrated at the points of departure and return, something you return to, to check in on. It is not just about bringing in a new force but also about being able to not know. Not knowing is not necessarily a deficiency;

it's patience, a reason to invest effort and envision possibilities, the patience to know that it will entail negotiation and relation building, but also fear that you're not doing something right or fear that you will get it wrong. I think, when you have care, fear is diluted because the foundation is firmly set.

Going back to something that has been echoed repeatedly, the foundation of colonialism is exploitation, and these structures have not healed or have not been addressed sufficiently. Care is what fills in the cracks and negotiates healing in the work, in the sense that transformation has a healing component. You learn when to integrate the intentionality to move in directions you've not been before. It's negotiating, approaching, and diving in. Being open to try, leading with care and grace. Rhythmic alignment and misalignment happens, right? So when misalignments are happening, if you have a spirit of care in the exploration and dedication to the work, then the fluidity will be there. End of my draft.

BARKER When we talk about care and safe spaces, I come back to values, a value system, and value-based work. You need patience, humility—even if you're working with someone you have an issue with. You have to breathe, listen, and acknowledge your partner, like in acting. The nature of the work we do is connecting with people. So we do Pathways, which Mūkonzi mentioned, and identify anything that could be an issue. We have a bunch of people read it because everyone has blind spots. Then, if one person says, "That's not a problem," but another goes, "Yeah, no, that's going to be a problem," we acknowledge it and then we have an idea of how to address it. That's all prerehearsal orientation: talking to people about the work and then changing the way we do rehearsals based on what's needed. What I often find with institutions is they show up in many ways, and, because

Vern Thiessen's *The Diviners.* Photo: David Hou

of our Equity agreements and legal guidelines for how we work together, they say, "We get there and start working. It's eight hours. You're called this day. I'm called this day. It's this work. Do the work!" And for us, it's actually slowing it down. That's how care happens. You have to breathe and—like Mūkonzi said—everything is present in the moment. Sometimes when you're directing a show, you have a great plan but within five minutes you have to throw it out because the people in front of you don't fit that plan. Care has to be the same way, because if someone suddenly has very strong emotions about something, we have to address it, which is why we also make sure that there are resources available for everyone.

When I'm in a room with people, some things can feel overwhelming. That idea of checking in at the beginning of the day . . . sometimes our bodies arrive and our spirits arrive after. Then at the end of the day, I find doing a checkout really helps people land. We say, "Leave that baggage at the door and come in and do the work." But that baggage is always in the room. We always sense these things. Like Mūkonzi says, we adapt the room to what's happening. Checking out at

Audience members at Schauspielhaus Zürich's Pfauenbühne, Zurich, Switzerland, 2024. Photo: T+T Photo, Juliet Haller

the end of the day, it's about leaving it in the room. Trying to teach people how to let it go, to leave it in the room and walk away.

To me, it's always about the work. How are we working together? How are we taking care of each other?

DIOH For the institution, we have legally binding forms of care. We have to take care of our employees. We try to figure out what actions of care are needed on different levels of the institution. We came to realize that not every department needs the same forms of care. It depends on the job. Schauspielhaus Zürich has something between 300 and 350 employees and around seventy different jobs. The technical staff has a different workday than the artistic staff, the administrative staff, or stage management. So, beyond the legalized forms of care we cannot change, we need to figure out what people need more concretely. I think we came to realize that for many people care was about communication. It's not even so much about these safer spaces. A lot of people want them, but a lot of people just want to be able to communicate.

One larger thing we did on the level of HR was structured conflict management. Conflict management has a certain routine; it's people with the specific competencies doing it. So it doesn't have to be this weird, "Oh, we have a conflict there. Just talk to the director or talk to this person," which might not be helpful or de-escalating for people without the institutional legitimacy to do it. A lot of people need this kind of institution-sanctioned "This is the person I go to. This is the person I trust to do the job. I don't want to talk with random people. I don't want to have to find the solution myself." I feel like this is especially the case for conflicts that arise from sexism, racism, or any other form of discrimination. You need this very clear route to "This happened to me. I need to be able to go somewhere and it has to be clear who I'm going to." This was a big part of institutionalizing questions of care.

The other thing is, Zurich always acts like it's a big city, but it's really not. We don't even have half a million people, but we act as if we're very big. We're very connected, which has positive and negative sides. It can be tricky. We try to encourage people to find moments of joy. It sounds very kitsch, but it's not always easy to find the structural answers to care. What we can control is creating these beautiful moments amongst each other. I also think it's good to find people outside theater and outside Zurich . . . although Zurich is actually not that easy to come to from the outside, and the theater bubble is very, very tight and crosses with the academic bubble. . . . They intersect very easily. But we have to find moments of joy together. It's very important to see the collectivity in care. I feel like especially in theater contexts, it is so important to really emphasize the collectivity of it.

It can be very fruitful to take care of someone, but also to receive it—like the reciprocity that Mūkonzi mentioned. I do a lot of talks one-on-one, just conversations. That's part of my job. They don't have to result in anything. They're just talks. If you want me to do something, I will. But they're just a conversation. This helped us a lot to, like you said, Keith, understand the moods, conditions, and context of people coming into work. We still have a long way to go, especially in other departments, because we are notorious for our levels of exhaustion and need to figure out the care question.

VANDEN THOREN We try to facilitate the importance of peers with the Social Fund. We bring together people with shared experiences and try to create moments where we can heal together. We try to facilitate moments of joy in a safe space. We stress the importance of external trust—in Belgium, organizations can hire external confidential contact persons to mediate when necessary or be a sympathetic ear—and shared experiences. We promote the check-ins and checkouts to try to slow down, because it's a very high-paced environment. That's what we do in terms of care.

CLIMENHAGA *One last question: What do your institutions need to look like in ten years from your perspective?*

VANDEN THOREN Decentralized.

DIOH I would hope that in ten years, they don't need my job anymore, because everybody understands what they need to do.

BARKER I would say, these things we're talking about, I would love it if they were actually embedded in the practice, as opposed to something that's brought in.

BRASCOUPÉ I would say having diversity and inclusion as a core tenet of what we do, and that it's one of the very first things we think about and not something that we add on afterwards.

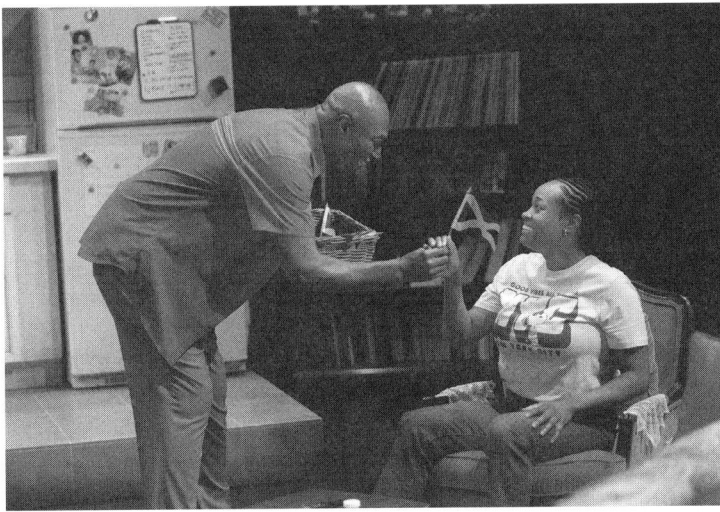

MŪSYOKI I would say to be something that is not an ongoing work but part of the nucleus. Part of the core. Something that is not top down or bottom up, just everywhere. No one is feeling like they're not relevant, no one is feeling they need to leave, no one is feeling threatened. They feel that feeling of a kid dancing in the rain. You know that feeling? Yes. End of my draft.

Andrea Scott's *Get That Hope*, Stratford Festival, Stratford, Ontario, 2024. Photo: David Hou

NOAH LENA VERCAUTEREN

INSTITUTIONALIZED COLLECTIVITY/ COLLECTIVES IN INSTITUTIONS IN FLANDERS AND THE NETHERLANDS

After a financial and cultural crisis where it was on the verge of losing essential subsidies, a collective of collectives took up artistic direction at Toneelhuis, the Flemish city theater in Antwerp, Belgium, in 2022. This direction consisted of three artists and two collectives, all of which were directly connected to the city theater as part of its open ensemble. A year later, NTGent, the city theater in Ghent, Belgium, put out a call for a new artistic direction to follow up Swiss German director Milo Rau, explicitly allowing both individuals and collectives to apply.[1] After reviewing several candidates, the theater chose a three-headed artistic direction.[2] While perhaps seen as a radical (political) decision, the roots of these situations can be traced back to the strong emergence of the practice of collective theater-making in the 1960s, which has marked the theater landscape of Flanders (the Dutch-speaking region of Belgium) and the Netherlands. Just like other practices that were once radical, working collectively has become incredibly commonplace and in some ways institutionalized. However, while the Netherlands and Flanders share this history, the ways in which collectivity and collectives have become institutionalized, in particular when it comes to institutional leadership, differ greatly. Understanding the different outcomes of the same collective history, and why and how they can diverge, can help with understanding its political consequences and possibilities and give insight into the question of whether a collective institutional dramaturgy is starting to dig its roots into the Western theater soil.

The Flemish and Dutch theater fields can be seen as a connected though not fully homogeneous field. Both areas share the same language and have significant crossover in their theater landscapes, more than Belgium has internally between Dutch-speaking Flanders and French-speaking Wallonia. This is not just a linguistic border but also a

Toneelhuis Season Presentation 2024–25, The Boourla Theatre, Toneelhuis, Antwerp, Belgium, 2024. Photo: Monday Agbonzee Jr.

Theater 55:2   DOI 10.1215/01610775-11683585

legislative one, as Dutch and French theater systems have been separated through policy and subsidies since 1954.[3] Flemish theater needs to program shows across the borders of its small region to be economically viable, so it is only natural that it has formed close connections with the only other neighboring country that shares its language.[4] The Flemish and Dutch theater landscapes also share an important cultural evolution: the emergence of theater collectives in the 1960s.

Influenced by a sociocultural climate of student protests, international theater collectives, and years of growing social restlessness, theater-makers in the Netherlands and Flanders started realizing more and more that they did not want to work in the hierarchical institutions anymore; rather, they wanted to work in a hyperhorizontal, democratic structure.[5] Further emboldened by the artistic-political action of Aktie Tomaat in 1969, a protest where two theater students threw tomatoes at the stage after a showing of Shakespeare's *The Tempest* by the city theater of Amsterdam, a number of young theater-makers banded together in collectives to react to what they perceived as a crisis in theater. There was no structural support for avant-garde theater, meaning only the big subsidized theater institutions had a say in what was being produced.[6] An open discussion on November 1, 1969, between theater-makers and the city theater led nowhere.[7] According to a new generation of theater-makers, the only place that *could* support new theater was forsaking their duty to the cultural field.[8] So they took it upon themselves to become a new space for cultural development.

The rise of theater collectives in the following years became a strong counterinstitutional practice. Whereas the large institutions worked with fixed ensembles and clear, separate roles (e.g., directors, actors, scenographers, and technicians), the new collectives worked with a radically horizontal structure. Working collectively influenced every part of the working process: choosing and reading texts, working out a scenography, administration, and logistics. Theater was done collectively on every level.[9] The biggest example for this collective practice in the Flemish Dutch field became and still is Maatschappij Discordia, centered around theater-maker Jan Joris Lamers. While not all collectives work as radically, the idea that everyone shares an equal part in the creating process has influenced many theater-makers to this day, with new collectives like Camping Sunset (Belgium) and Club Lam (the Netherlands) still responding to issues in the field with collective work. In an overview chapter on Flemish Dutch theater collectives, Kati Röttger even posits that it is precisely the poetics of collectivity that makes Flemish and Dutch theater stand out.[10] Its counterinstitutional practice also led to the rise of smaller theaters thriving in major cities in the Netherlands and Belgium. Places like Shaffytheater in Amsterdam or Nieuwpoortteater in Ghent became breeding grounds for new artists to experiment with these new aesthetics.[11] Many of these collectives and volunteer-led initiatives have by now become institutionalized and/or subsidized, or they have disappeared after losing structural support.[12] Despite the institutionalization of some of these entities, they still hold a fringe status in the landscape

and predominantly program new and experimental work, all made possible by state subsidies that keep commercial concerns at bay. They have also maintained a relatively flexible nature. Whenever structural subsidies have been cut, the lost collectives and structures are not always mourned, as artists continuously come together and disband in new collectives and structures. This shows that it is the collective *practice*, not the collective *entity*, that is the most important.

The practice and aesthetics of collectivity remain one of the strong connections between Flanders and the Netherlands, as a lot of collectives today are composed of both Flemish and Dutch artists. However, while it remains a counterinstitutional practice for many new theater-makers in the Netherlands, collectivity as an artistic practice, as opposed to classic director-actor relations, has become more institutionalized in Flanders. The reason for this might lie in the specific Flemish phenomenon of the "Flemish wave," a term for a perceived aesthetic shift in the Flemish arts in the 1970s and 1980s from classic theater to what will later be called postdramatic theater and dance, with artists such as Jan Decorte and Sigrid Vinks, Anne Teresa De Keersmaeker, and collectives such as tg STAN deconstructing what theater and dance can be. The personal legacies of many of these artists have become tainted in recent years, as testimonies of harassment and bad working conditions have come to light, but the aesthetic shift has been a permanent one. While the first collectives in the 1970s were

Lo van Hensbergen accuses an actor at the Aktie Tomaat meeting, November 1, 1969, The Stadsschouwburg, Amsterdam, Netherlands. Photo: Pieter Boersma

Aktie Tomaat meeting, November 1, 1969, The Stadsschouwburg, Amsterdam, Netherlands, 1969. Photo: Pieter Boersma

interested in working with alternative repertoire, Flemish theater-makers during and after the Flemish wave were only marginally interested in repertoire, and if they were, they wanted to deconstruct it completely.[13] Instead, participative practices, improvisation, and devised theater became the center of artistic production, with actor-director constellations being replaced by more artistic cocreative structures. Even the Flemish theater institutions had to start following the example of these new aesthetics to stay relevant.[14] The "avant-garde" became the institutional center, even if it was still called "avant-garde."[15] With a changed landscape, Flemish theaters did not need a large ensemble anymore to stage repertoire plays and evolved toward open, fluid ensembles, consisting of performers, theater-makers, and collectives, unlike Dutch theaters like Internationaal Theater Amsterdam (ITA) and Het Nationale Theater (HNT), who still work with fixed ensembles. While some Dutch theaters, such as Theater Rotterdam, have very recently switched to an open ensemble, Flanders has not had a single institutional ensemble since 2017, when NTGent, the city theater of Ghent, under Milo Rau switched to an open ensemble, over a decade later than the two other city theaters. The aftermath of the Flemish wave, strengthened by the current neoliberal climate of flexible freelance work, has resulted in a Flemish theater landscape of theater-makers and performers more interested in working in horizontal collectives than in vertical institutions.[16] It is no surprise, then, that Flemish theater institutions, influenced by the Flemish wave and the history of collectives, and already with the tendency to step away from the traditional, have taken steps toward institutionalized collective practices in the form of collective leadership. In the connected field of Flanders and the Netherlands, it is this difference that shows a hint of a national border.

The timing for the emergence of collective leadership in the Flemish field is not a total coincidence. Collectives seem always to pop up in times of artistic and/or political crisis.[17] Rau initially came to NTGent as part of a three-headed leadership, but once his term started, the collective dissolved into a single leadership. The first full experiment in collective leadership then, as noted above, came out of the artistic and financial crisis of the Antwerp city theater, Toneelhuis. Finding the right person to follow up artistic director Guy Cassiers, who had had the position for sixteen years, had been a tumultuous process.[18] This type of "crisis of succession" often happens in these cases, as Christopher Balme has discussed.[19] When in 2022 the new direction, consisting of a shared leadership of three women, seemed to be responsible for potentially losing vital structural subsidies, the crisis only worsened and became one not just of succession but of impending financial doom.[20] A collective leadership of three artists and two collectives was a temporary answer, as the artists attempted to save themselves independently in this crisis. This later became the permanent solution.[21] A year later, this experiment had clearly influenced at least one other institution, with NTGent following suit and appointing a collective artistic leadership, this time consisting of three people carrying the title of "artistic director," while at Toneelhuis currently eight people hold that title. Interestingly, this time collective leadership arose not out of a large crisis but out of a relatively normal process of succession. This potentially shows a more institutional change toward collectivity, just as the later theater collectives were a sign of an embedded practice, after the revolution.

While *shared* leadership is not uncommon in the West, *collective* leadership more clearly has its roots in the history of collective practice and is not just an answer to more global calls to rethink neoliberal individualism. Institutions being led by more than one director is nothing new. The division of leadership between different responsibilities has been a solution, employed in many different institutions, to deal with the otherwise overwhelming demands of leading big structures. A new wave in institutional critique has also forced many to reconsider the position of institutions, what can be changed *in* institutions, and whether it is in any way logical for so many responsibilities and that amount of influence in a theater institution to fall on one person.[22] As Balme notes, the "charismatic leadership" model is experiencing a crisis in German theater.[23] Furthermore, in his article on the possibilities and problems of shared leadership, Alexander Keil aptly points out that performer-director dependence is weakened in the case of a team of directors, as there are multiple entry points for performers to find a way into the institution.[24] What has already happened in institutions in the UK

Exterior of NTGent Schouwburg, NTGent, Ghent, Belgium. Photo: Michiel Devijer

and German theater is a sort of coleadership, with two people sharing the total responsibility by dividing it into manageable parts. I would like to argue that this is different from collective leadership, a type of leadership where the practice of collectivity is at the center of the way responsibility is shared. Where shared leadership divides the responsibility, collective leadership attempts at truly sharing it.

As Röttger points out with theater collectives, not everything that coexists is necessarily done collectively.[25] The practice of collectivity, in the way that the Flemish Dutch theater collectives pursue it, tried to go beyond coexistence. If it is about managing the theater in a more efficient way, where responsibilities and fields can be divided among more people, the shared leadership model is more about efficient and compartmentalized leadership than about instituting collectivity. In theaters like ITA and various German theaters, we see this in the different titles the directors get (artistic, creative, and managing) or the clear distinction in artistic expertise (i.e., theater vs. dance). Collective leadership, such as the current artistic direction at Toneelhuis, NTGent, and already in 2017 at Theaterhaus Jena (Germany) with the appointment of Dutch theater collective Wunderbaum, tries to institute collectivity by giving a group of people the same responsibility. In a theater where the implementation and subsequent institutionalization of collectivity is put at the forefront, the importance of multiple voices within an institution seems to be highlighted. Having this polyphony at the highest level of an institution could potentially more accurately represent the diversity of the theater's audience.[26] Collectivity, in that case, is a tool that might actually hinder institutional efficiency, but follows the democratic principles that the Flemish Dutch theater collectives put forward. It is the philosophy of the collectivity of theater-making that is present here. It is also only possible if the ruling belief is that a conversation, and the possibility of dissent when competing voices talk on the same subject, can be a form of leadership and can be valuable for the institutional dramaturgy of a city theater. In a sense, it is a response not just to a leadership crisis but to an institutional crisis.

Toneelhuis and NTGent each work slightly differently when it comes to the sharing of institutional responsibility. In the case of Toneelhuis, a revolving scheme ensures that each part of the leading collective can leave their mark. Online they are all credited individually as artistic director, even while some of them are also part of a separate theater collective.[27] Most public-facing acts, such as the presentation of the new season, are done collectively, with the artists of the collectives Olympique Dramatique and FC Bergman representing both their role as part of the collective direction and their role as part of a theater collective. In 2024, at the public presentation of the new season, this resulted in a scenography of a dinner table onstage, where all artists sat together and interviewed each other about their upcoming work and the season to come for an audience sitting in the dark. The new artists in residence for the coming season were briefly invited to sit with them, and performances formed intermezzos and gave a taste of the dramaturgy of the season. The upcoming season consists of productions indicative of each artist's artistic voice (Lisaboa Houbrechts takes on a classic Brecht play, while Gorges Ocloo

: WE START FROM THE END IS WHERE
IEDEREEN
WELKOM

further develops his format of the AfrOpera), but also an added effort to radically open up the institution to a minority group that has historically been neglected in Flanders: the deaf and hard-of-hearing community, with a Flemish Sign Language adaptation of Chekhov's *The Seagull* as innovative artistic and institutional choice. As a format this presentation is somewhat traditional, as it is staged in a theater auditorium with a seated audience, but what happens onstage carries the aesthetic of collective decision-making and the need for an openness to the audience—even a future audience, as the presentation prominently featured two sign language interpreters and featured an audio description at the start for the whole audience. The presentation of the new season was everyone's responsibility, with no divisions according to genre or part of the program (e.g., own productions, guest artists, new development, etc.), thus staging collective leadership within a frame of open discussion at a dinner table. While the audience could not join, its "side" at the table was not occupied and remained open.

The collective artistic leadership at NTGent is now starting its first full season, after a transition period from Milo Rau to the current trio. All three carry the title of artistic director, but instead of a revolving scheme, each has a different "role": the role of maker, the role of curator, and the role of artistic developer, with two out of the three also producing their own work at the city theater.[28] While boundaries between

Toneelhuis Season Presentation 2024–25. Photo: Monday Agbonzee Jr.

the three are there, these delineations are based on artistic roles rather than differing institutional responsibilities (i.e., artistic vs. managing) or disciplines (i.e., theater vs. dance). Again, the scenography of their new season's presentation tries to convey an institutional dramaturgy of open collectivity: after a brief introduction from two of the three artistic directors, the new city dramaturg and a programmer, audience members were invited to sit at tables with sharing plates and listen to people from the artistic team talk about the new season. The team changed tables after a set time, allowing audience members to stay seated and enjoy the food while different productions (both original as well as guest productions) where introduced. In contrast with Toneelhuis, the audience was invited to join and talk directly with members of the artistic team, potentially challenging the decisions they had made. The interaction between the artistic direction, however, was not explicitly visible in the presentation, unlike with Toneelhuis, which had allowed a (staged) look into collective conversations within the institution. The content of the new season, interestingly, does not signal a complete change in artistic profile, a phenomenon that can often happen in theaters, as new leadership can bring with it a complete change in creative team.[29] Instead, it is a mixture of usual productions, such as Lara Staal's social projects, the *Histoire(s) du théâtre* series originated by Rau, and new work by two of the three artistic directors (Yves Degryse with his collective Berlin and Barbara Raes). Externally, then, the new

Aktie Tomaat meeting, November 1, 1969. Photo: Pieter Boersma

collective leadership in NTGent is not presented as an answer to a crisis, even when it logically stands in contrast with the leadership model under Rau. It is not shown as a revolutionary act, which means perhaps that it can be an institutional act of change.

Both NTGent and Toneelhuis try to present themselves as more diverse, open, and democratic through this type of collective leadership. What the collective leadership and its public presentations seem to connect with is the desire for an institutional openness. Coincidentally, the symbol of a dinner table (or multiple) connects the public presentation of both institutional dramaturgies, in Antwerp and in Ghent. It breaks with the typical format of a season's presentation, where the audience is being spoken to by an artistic director and a number of artists and employees. The need to present the coming season of the institution in this way shows a desire to connect with the aesthetics and practice of open collectivity. Still, when we consider the institution outside of this public presentation, the need to differentiate internally in some capacity remains, for which the reason potentially lies in the rigidity of institutional structures, where employees and artists still need to know who to turn to for what and when. This need is solved at Toneelhuis by a kind of director's estafette, passing the responsibility from one to the next, while outwardly always representing the house as a collective. At NTGent, the role division is supposed to bring clarity to the collective direction. Either way, both examples show experiments in leadership that go beyond shared leadership and try to embody collectivity.

For both NTGent and Toneelhuis, however, there are aspects of the theater collective philosophy that cannot really be maintained, such as truly radical horizontal processes and the "polygamy" of artists.[30] While the artists within the artistic direction are technically free to make work in other places, they do carry the status of artistic director with them. Even if a new production might align more with fringe aesthetics, their strong institutional connection makes a true flexible career nearly impossible. Because of institutional rigidity, it is also harder to follow the fluidity that can come with collective horizontal practices, as institutions cannot dissolve and come together in new structures as easily. Whereas collectives could flow, institutions would break. The term *collective leadership* can also be easily critiqued as a contradictory term in the context of Flemish Dutch theater collectives. Responsibility is not shared throughout the whole institution in a truly collective way, as it is hard to imagine that someone from the artistic direction will work a shift at the ticketing office or that everyone in the whole institution can have a direct say in the institutional dramaturgy of the city theater. While it attempts at institutionalized polyphony at the highest level, it does not deconstruct institutional hierarchies as radically as the Flemish Dutch theater collectives did.

In conclusion, the practice of collectivity that has been cultivated for years, alongside changes in Flemish institutional dramaturgies after the Flemish wave, is resulting in new modes of collective leadership that differ from shared leadership in interesting ways. Whether this type of leadership truly leads to an open, democratic institution is not yet clear. It is still a hierarchical structure, albeit less individual. Although the institutions try to offer chairs at the table, it is still clear who decides how the table is set. The future will reveal whether this type of leadership in Flanders is the start of a radical institutional dramaturgy in Europe and can be the answer to the crisis of succession,[31] or whether it is just a temporary leadership experiment. However, as Keil argues, any alternative brings more insight into possible solutions.[32] It potentially carries a strong message in an international landscape that is prone to personality cults. Ideally, these attempts at institutional(ized) collectivity signal a move toward an understanding of the institution as a collective entity, not just the ship of one (seemingly charismatic) captain.

Notes

1. "Vacancies," NTGent, https://www.ntgent.be/en/vacancies (accessed June 2, 2023).

2. "Yves Degryse, Barbara Raes en Melih Gençboyaci worden nieuwe artistieke leiding," NTGent, July 4, 2023, https://www.ntgent.be/nl/nieuws/yves-degryse-barbara-raes-en-melih-gen%C3%A7boyaci-worden-nieuwe-artistieke-leiding.

3. Luk Van den Dries, "Belgium," in *Theatre Worlds in Motion: Structures, Politics and Developments in the Countries of Western Europe*, ed. Hans van Maanen and S. E. Wilmer (Amsterdam: Rodopi, 1998), 76.

4. Simon Leenknegt, "Vlaamse podiumkunsten: Een internationaal drama in 5 aktes," *Kunstenpunt*, April 20, 2017, https://www.kunsten.be/nu-in-de-kunsten/vlaamse-podiumkunsten-een-internationaal-drama-in-5-aktes/; Joris Janssens, "Vijfentwintig problemen met de internationale spreiding van theater en dans," *Kunstenpunt*, March 22, 2017, https://www.kunsten.be/nu-in-de-kunsten/25-problemen-met-de-internationale-spreiding-van-theater-en-dans/.

5. Kati Röttger, "Theatercollectieven in Nederland: Theorie, context en historie sinds de jaren '60. van sociaal (ont)waken naar sociaal werken," in *de collectieven: Een unieke theatergeschiedenis*, ed. Constant Meijers (Amsterdam: Uitgeverij it&fb, 2022), 14–15.

6. Max van Engen, "Begin van de Aktie Tomaat: De crisis in het theater leidt tot openlijk protest en acties van het publiek," in *Een theatergeschiedenis der Nederlanden: Tien eeuwen drama en theater in Nederland en Vlaanderen*, ed. Robert Lambertus Erenstein (Amsterdam: Amsterdam University Press, 1996), 754.

7. Hans Smit and Eva Smit, "Zomerspecial: Aktie Tomaat—de 1 november discussie," *Theaterkrant*, August 25, 2019, https://www.theaterkrant.nl/podcast/zomerspecial-aktie-tomaat-de-1-november-discussie-deel-1/.

8. Van Engen, "Begin van de Aktie Tomaat," 758.

9. Röttger, "Theatercollectieven in Nederland," 30.

10. Röttger, "Theatercollectieven in Nederland," 23.

11. Nan van Houte, "Felix meritis: Broedplaats van collectief theater," in *de collectieven: Een unieke theatergeschiedenis*, ed. Constant Meijers (Amsterdam: Uitgeverij it&fb, 2022), 76.

12. Robbert van Heuven, "De opkomst van het kleinezaalcircuit," in *de collectieven: Een unieke theatergeschiedenis*, ed. Constant Meijers (Amsterdam: Uitgeverij it&fb, 2022), 60.

13. Wouter Hillaert, "Pflegen und Mästen. // Nursing and Feeding," *Theater der Zeit spezial*, 2013, 35.

14. Erwin Jans, *Drie stadstheaters op zoek naar hun toekomst* (Antwerp: Bebuquin/Toneelhuis, 2023), https://toneelhuis.be/nl/post/drie-stadstheaters-op-zoek-naar-hun-toekomst/.

15. Jan Goossens, "The Endless Possibilities of a City-Theatre: KVS 2001–2015," in *Turn, Turtle! Reenacting the Institute*, ed. Elke van Campenhout and Lilia Mestre (Berlin: Alexander Verlag, 2016), 27.

16. Kristof Van Baarle, "After the Wave, the Flood? Finding a New Autonomy and Relation to Work," *Arts* 11, no. 4 (2022): 74, https://doi.org/10.3390/arts11040074.

17. Röttger, "Theatercollectieven in Nederland," 38.

18. Ewoud Ceulemans, "Onrust in Toneelhuis: Geen opvolger voor Guy Cassiers, morrend personeel," *De Morgen*, November 7, 2019, https://www.demorgen.be/nieuws/onrust-in-toneelhuis-geen-opvolger-voor-guy-cassiers-morrend-personeel~bdd66b33/.

19. Christopher Balme, "Die Krise der Nachfolge: Zur Institutionalisierung charismatischer Herrschaft im deutschen Stadt- und Staatstheater," *Zeitschrift für Kulturmanagement und Kulturpolitik* 5, no. 2 (2019): 43, https://doi.org/10.14361/zkmm-2019-0203.

20. Karl van den Broeck, "Toneelhuis vecht voor zijn leven en niemand ligt er wakker van," *Apache*, May 6, 2022, https://apache.be/2022/05/06/toneelhuis-vecht-voor-zijn-leven-en-niemand-ligt-er-wakker-van.

21. "Collectief van theatermakers gaat Toneelhuis leiden," *De Standaard*, September 8, 2022, https://www.standaard.be/cnt/dmf20220908_95933334.

22. Andrea Fraser, "From the Critique of Institutions to an Institution of Critique," *Artforum*, September 2005, https://www.artforum.com/features/from-the-critique-of-institutions-to-an-institution-of-critique-172201/; Alexander Keil, "Intendant: In sein ist schwer, als Co-Leitung zu arbeiten noch viel mehr," *Versus: Magazin für kritische Organisationspraxis*, May 30, 2024, https://versus-online-magazine.com/de/artikel/coleitung-theater/.

23. Balme, "Die Krise der Nachfolge," 38.

24. Keil, "Intendant: In sein ist schwer."

25. Röttger, "Theatercollectieven in Nederland," 11.

26. Keil, "Intendant:in sein ist schwer."

27. "Wie is wie," Toneelhuis, https://toneelhuis.be/nl/wie-is-wie/ (accessed September 9, 2024).

28. "Yves Degryse, Barbara Raes en Melih Gençboyaci worden nieuwe artistieke leiding."

29. Balme, "Die Krise der Nachfolge," 39.

30. Röttger, "Theatercollectieven in Nederland," 35.

31. Balme, "Die Krise der Nachfolge," 53.

32. Keil, "Intendant: In sein ist schwer."

Puri Senja's *The Other Half: 27 Déjà Vu*, OpenLab Presentation, Teater Garasi, Kasihan, Indonesia, 2021. Courtesy of Teater Garasi

Ugoran Prasad

Toward a Street-Level, Postterritory Dramaturgy

Perspectives from Garasi Performance Institute

Decentralizing Institutional Dramaturgy

I would like to explore a specific, contextually informed interpretation of the term *institutional dramaturgy* for Indonesian theater. My attempt to apply the term, as theorized and historically mapped by Katalin Trencsényi, as a lens requires me to think of institutional infrastructure and apparatus in a completely different configuration.[1] I propose locating the Garasi Performance Institute, the performance hub where I work, as an agent and part of a continuum of institutional knowledge transmission in Indonesian theater. I propose that theater groups have served as the most persistent theater institutions and the primary producer of theater culture in Indonesia since, at the very least, the end of the 1960s. Within this landscape, institutional dramaturgy occurs twice over. First, the institutional dramaturgies of influential theater groups become a model and reference for theater practice at large; and, second, theater groups, tactical in nature, sustain or alter their institutional structure to respond or intervene with a certain exteriority.

A case should be made to discuss several key institutions as strong support systems for theater practice: for example, festivals, independent funding bodies, and so on. Similarly, a separate critique is necessary to demonstrate how the state and its funding mechanisms have primarily hindered rather than facilitated artistic freedom over the past fifty years—how cultural disobedience became the shared value of Indonesian theater. But I limit the scope of this writing to the viewpoint of what Michel de Certeau defined as the street level: space-making tactical institutions working from the absence of a place proper.[2] From the ongoing findings of that street level, in the final part of this article I aim to discuss how Garasi's recent experiment in institutional dramaturgy signals a shift toward the post–theater group, postterritorial epistemologies.

Theater 55:2 DOI 10.1215/01610775-11683598

At the turn of the twenty-first century, the Teater Garasi Foundation was initially established as an institutional support for Teater Garasi—an emerging theater group working in Yogyakarta since 1993. The foundation has been operating as a cultural organization, with social and cultural programs predominantly far removed from the theater stage—the furthest backstage of our theater-making front. While it could not directly support our theatrical works, it provided working infrastructure—from the office, the library, and the audiovisual and physical studio—pivotal to our works.[3] Over the years, our theatricality has permeated many of our social programs (workshops, symposiums, forums, etc.)—our actors have inhabited and taken certification for organizational roles such as treasurer, librarian, or archivist. On the night of August 31, 2021, however, the rare occasion emerged for our institutional dramaturgy to bluntly (and overdramatically, at times) appear on our front stage.[4]

PERFORMING CROSSROADS

On August 31, 2021, Garasi Performance Institute presented *Performing Crossroads: Precarious Reflection on the Margins* to a limited audience in our studio in Yogyakarta, Indonesia.[5] The performance was commissioned by 25 Years 25 Hours, an online festival celebrating the twenty-fifth anniversary of the Prince Claus Fund, a Dutch-based foundation for culture and development.[6] Ong Keng Sen, the festival curator, invited us to share our works (performance and cultural programs), particularly those from the period after we received the Prince Claus Awards in 2013. The eventual performance we devised was based on sections of our official program descriptions and proposals, which were then juxtaposed with individual stories, reflections, and field notes from our collective labors since 2017 (this year was chosen for reasons I will explore below). Some projects, such as the *Multitude of Peer Gynts* project (2018–21) and the *Performing*

Teater Garasi's *Performing Crossroads: Precarious Reflection on the Margins*, Kasihan, Indonesia, 2021. Courtesy of Teater Garasi

Difference program (2017–18), took more stage time than others. The first was a transnational performance project between artists from Japan, Sri Lanka, and Indonesia, while the latter was a cultural and knowledge exchange program between Garasi and local performance-makers in four satellite cities in peripheralized locations in Indonesia.

The commission was staged during the limbo of the COVID-19 years. That night, we tried to make sense of our present time through the not-so-distant past. A few days before that, on August 27, we had concluded the last part of our *Multitude of Peer Gynts* project as an online theater event. As for many other conventional theater-makers during that time, an emergency refuge in the virtual space was, at the very least, dreamlike, if not nightmarish. The undercurrent of those heightened times was the total inability to fathom a tomorrow, and somehow it awakened poetry in unlikely places: reports, documents, transcripts, proposals, receipts, and spreadsheets. At Garasi Performance Institute, we have long been aware of the importance of developing a healthy institution as the shoulder of our aesthetic practice—particularly in this COVID period, we could anticipate questions about health standards and measurement.

Performing Crossroads documents the ongoing shift in our institutional approach that began in 2017 when we started exploring a new institutional form that moved away from the artist-collective theater group form we had maintained for a decade. There are several reasons for this change. Internally, one key factor was that the individual development and professional trajectories of some of our collective members prevented them from taking active roles in the collective project, especially as they relocated to other cities, either within or outside Indonesia. Second, there is always an aspect of self-centeredness when working to advance a theater group. The idea of progress, or what is cautioned by Walter Benjamin as "the storm," has become more problematic as we march through these decades, especially as we arrive at the other end of the recent pandemic.[7] Outside the group, we sensed a shifting trend in the theater-making approach of major cities, where more productions are attributed to individuals rather than theater groups. Meanwhile, peripheralized cities have new collectives working on exciting topics while temporarily reclaiming various social places for theater stages. The mutable nature of institutional forms was familiar. We understood that the theater group—and any citizen organization—is subject to external influences and part of a constantly evolving social landscape. Over the last fifty years, this mutable nature has opened diverse models for theater groups.

History and Context

Since 1968, the Indonesian theater has seen different experiments with diverse institutional dramaturgies and formats. Rendra's Bengkel Teater, Arifin C. Noer's Teater Kecil, and, half a decade later, Putu Wijaya's Teater Mandiri introduced a model in which the theater group acts as a sociocultural refuge and learning space for members from diverse backgrounds.[8] Bengkel Teater was highly invested in adopting and tailoring the *sanggar* system—a system developed in Indonesia since the 1920s that entailed coworking and coliving—for experimental theater practice, the most dominant paradigm in Indonesian theater.[9] Bengkel closely structured its members' physical routines, introducing different physical training models from Jawanese meditation to hybrid martial arts training. While also a space for actor development, Teater Kecil in Jakarta unintentionally operated like an informal schooling center for many aspiring theater directors, such as Nano Riantiarno and Boedi S. Otong. Nano would form

Teater Koma in 1977, exploring and expanding the Brechtian-like epic aesthetic of Teater Kecil even further. Koma was an exception, if not an anomaly, a rare model of a theater group that captured the imagination of much of Jakarta's middle-class audience right up until today. Boedi took over Teater Sae in 1978 and paved the way for creating a trajectory for experimental physical theater throughout the 1980s and 1990s.[10] These groups would experiment with group format and *sanggar* system tailored to their aesthetic trajectories. Teater Koma would become more a group of a large number of performers and technicians, in contrast to Teater Sae's close-knit, nuclear family–like structure.

The absence of a national theater project as a unifying strategic organization has placed these theater groups at the forefront of theater institutionalization in Indonesia. The fact that there is no theater district or marketplace such as Broadway or West End in Indonesian cities—or in most other metropolitan cities in Asia—has placed further significance on theater groups as the primary institutional apparatus for sustaining theater culture. Within two decades, from the 1970s to the 1980s, it became evident that Indonesian theater practice at large had been unable to establish a sustainable economic relationship with its audience, as had been evident as early as 1971.[11] While exceptional cases such as Teater Koma and later Teater Gandrik do exist, the majority of theater groups would not view ticket sales as a viable means to cover production costs. After thirty years of operating, Garasi is still part of this majority. Theater-makers have become accustomed to exercising theater as a medium for artistic fulfillment and symbolic capital. Besides these two groups, most theater groups are accustomed to a very limited engagement, where three- or four-day runs are a luxury. Consequently, theater culture could not rely exclusively on public performances, prompting many groups to open their rehearsal spaces to invited audiences.

CHANGING NAMES, CHANGING MODELS

In many ways, Garasi merely continued to engage in the experimentation of the group format. In 2001, led by the founder and director Yudi Ahmad Tajudin, Garasi adopted the format of a director-led theater laboratory in a mold of Eugenio Barba's training system and as a continuation of Teater Sae's model. During this period, in most of our published documents, the group's name shifted from simply Teater Garasi to Teater Garasi: Laboratorium Penciptaan Teater (Laboratory of Theater Creation).

The laboratory model, led and closely monitored by Yudi, managed to facilitate the growth of its participants, all of whom eventually saw themselves as performance initiators and makers. From 2005 to 2009, Garasi had four theater directors and eight actors leading and producing their respective projects. As described above, from Rendra of Bengkel to Boedi of Sae, the existing theater group model was predominantly an institution that belonged to its sole director. For Garasi, this trend signaled a time to

OpenLab 2021–22,
Teater Garasi,
Kasihan, Indonesia,
2022. Courtesy of
Teater Garasi

experiment with a different institutional format. We adopted the artist-collective form because it promised a more equal relationship within the group, once again shifting the grammar of our institutional dramaturgy. It was within this period that Garasi's collective devised its Peripheral Trilogy: *Je.ja.l.an* (*The Street*; 2009), *Tubuh Ketiga* (*Third Body*; 2012), and *Yang Fana adalah Waktu* (*Time Is Transient*; 2015). It also facilitated a working laboratory for Jompet Kuswidananto's visual art project *Phantasmagoria* (2009–13) and Yennu Ariendra's sound and noise work *Raja Kirik*.[12]

In 2017, not long after identifying the need for another turn in our institutional dramaturgy, we changed our formal name to Teater Garasi / Garasi Performance Institute, indicating a transition from Garasi as a collective to something else, yet to be revealed behind the term *institute*. In 2021, the collective paradigm and grammar continued to inform our approach, as seen in *Performing Crossroads*. Sharing our latest experiment in institutional dramaturgy, the performance was designed to be narrated entirely from the lived experiences and reflections of each collective member performing onstage. All collective members—except for myself due to COVID-19 travel restrictions in Australia—were present: the late Gunawan Maryanto, Yudi Ahmad Tajudin, Lusia Neti, Ignatius Sugiarto, Yennu Ariendra, and Arsita Iswardhani.

The performance made visible the narrative from the backstage of our institution, but that narrative was in many ways partial. In a sense, even on that day, while change has been inevitable for some time, we had yet to fully grasp its shape. We knew what we were no longer but hardly knew what we should be. As we evaluated *Crossroads* in the aftermath, we started to consider how its dramaturgy signifies how deeply institutionalized we were to view theater from the group lens. Over the collective's long history, our connection with practice has been deeply mediated by the spatially distributed nature of the theater group model. We identify spatialized nature as territorial or tribalistic in the sense that group identification shapes Indonesian theater culture at large. Cooperation and collaboration are the norm between these groups, mirroring the general landscape of Indonesian cultural diversity, but thin barriers and frictions do exist. Departed from the increasing scarcity and precarity of resources in the performance field, from the global constringency of its bordered working terrains, we were interested in exploring possibilities beyond the territorialized imaginations.

THE FUTURE OF GARASI

The mutable nature of performance inquiries, at least on paper, would seemingly allow us to operate without the trappings of territorialization and tribalism found in theater-group practice. If not, there is always time for mistakes and failed experiments. As of writing, in a time of institutional transition, the hub, as I called the group at the start of this article, is still called Garasi Performance Institute. We have dropped Teater Garasi from the official name. As an entity, Teater Garasi continues to exist, but for now it is in an inactive and a dormant state.

In the second half of 2023, members of the Teater Garasi collective became the minority of participants of the Garasi Performance Institute's institutional meetings. By then the performance hub format had been exercised more intensively for almost two years. Aside from many individual independent makers, the meetings consist of representatives of various performance and arts collectives across Indonesia, from Jakarta, Yogyakarta, Bandung (West Java), Surakarta (Central Java), Makassar (South Sulawesi), Pamekasan (Madura), Denpasar (Bali), and Maumere (East Flores). Throughout the second half of the year, a series of institutional meetings sought to find the best institutional format and structure for the immediate future of our shared hub.

These individuals and collectives have been participating, initiating, and developing a few projects with Garasi since the end of 2021. Some of them were Garasi collaborators and partners in the projects of *Performing Crossroads*, as well as a few participants of Majelis Dramaturgi—a nonhierarchical forum founded in 2017 where various performance-makers develop their own projects while also serving as dramaturgs for each other.[13] A few participants of OpenLab—an open school for emerging performance-makers based on Majelis's methodology—have been the initiators and operators of this new institutional experiment. With this new network of artists and programmers, we have produced a few cultural and theater projects, from the inter-Asian performance laboratory Invisible Dance Exchange project (a collaboration with Mandeep Raikhy [India], Avni Sethi [Conflictorium, India], and the Goethe Institute) to the *Waktu batu*

Teater Garasi's *Performing Crossroads: Precarious Reflection on the Margins*, 2021. Courtesy of Teater Garasi

(*Time Stoned*) performances, and we took over a series of works-in-progress at the mini-festival Cabaret Chairil beginning in 2018.

In the meantime, their respective collectives have continued to flourish. Kahe Community in Maumere, East Flores, has become a leading example of a vibrant Indonesian collective, tilting the center of cultural activism far from Jakarta and Jawa to the eastern side of Indonesia. Lembana Artgrow, from the small village of Lembana forty minutes outside Pamekasan, has been running an annual festival called Babad Lembana that exercises local knowledge as its curatorial and organizing framework: *hajatan* (event), *long-nolongin* (labor as a future investment), and *karjeh* (grand work). Mirat Kolektif, an all-women theater collective from Surakarta, has been recovering Rukiyah, a part of erased women artists and activists from the official history, in a series of performance works over the past three years.

Across this dynamic but seemingly hectic configurations of artists and collectives, we discovered that our shared working principle is best recognized as a shift from an artist-centered approach to a programmatic one, moving from a focus on *who* to a focus on *what*. Identifying theater and performance as a means of knowledge-making, the hub serves as a node of knowledge circulation in the larger network of performance practice and research. In this framework, the hub serves as a facilitator for performance inquiries rather than as an institution for artists. In practice, one inquiry could fluidly cross a few categories of inquiries. Babad Lembana, for example, occupies at least three categories: performance and social celebration, performing city, and decolonizing festivals. Kahe, Lembana, and Mirat share various points of knowledge encounters, including their participatory inquiries on the mothers of their respective locale as the main performers of civic engagements and activism.

Exterior of Teater Garasi, Kasihan, Indonesia, 2024. Courtesy of Teater Garasi

Following emphasis inquiries, the next working principle is to explore the extent of the work-in-progress approach to performance. The legacy of the previous generation's approach to theater culture is to open their rehearsal space to as large an audience as possible. Since the beginning of the Cabaret Chairil minifestival project, the hub has seen a potential for knowledge building in sharing not-yet-finished and ongoing works with both performance-makers and audiences. In the gestural, the ongoing and becoming, and, especially, the not-yet, we dream a postterritory utopia as dreamed by Ernst Bloch and as recharged by José Esteban Muñoz.[14] Hence, the hub plans to develop and organize a biennial gathering, Festival Pertunjukan Belum-Sudah (Not-Yet-Performance Festival), in 2025 and 2027. The festival we aspire to is a street-level postterritorial space of border-crossing encounters between performance-makers from various places to exchange inquiries, findings, and work-in-progress performances and to imagine collaborations. Making it happen certainly requires wider involvement, even beyond our current postterritorial imagination.

Notes

1. Katalin Trencsényi, *Dramaturgy in the Making: A User's Guide for Theatre Practitioners* (London: Bloomsbury Methuen Drama, 2015), 3–30.

2. Michel de Certeau, *The Practice of Everyday Life*, trans. Steven Rendall (Berkeley: University of California Press, 2008), 34–39.

3. Michael H. Bodden, "Languages of Traumas, Bodies, and Myths: Learning to Speak Again in Post-1998 Indonesian Theatre" (unpublished ms., n.d.), 34.

4. We will eventually call the form of the work a collective lecture, especially as we reorganize, reframe, and expand parts of it—focusing solely on the *Multitude of Peer Gynts* part—and stage the result a year later in Skien, Norway; see "Roundabout a Standstill; or, A Broken Report of *Multitude of Peer Gynts'* Findings—Ibsen Conference," *Ibsen Scope* (blog), https://ibsenscope.com/performance/roundabout-a -standstill-or-a-broken-report-of-multitude-of-peer-gynts-findings/ (accessed October 18, 2024).

5. "Performing Crossroads—Precarious Reflection on the Margins—Teter Garasi | 25 Years 25 Hours," posted by Prince Claus Fund, December 13, 2021, 60 mins., https:// www.youtube.com/watch?v=ApNS08xWZf8.

6. "*25 Years 25 Hours*—Announcements—e-Flux," *E-Flux* (blog), accessed October 18, 2024, https://www.e-flux.com/announcements/428917/25-years-25-hours/.

7. Walter Benjamin, "Theses on the Philosophy of History," in *Illuminations* (New York: Houghton Mifflin Harcourt, 1968), 253–64.

8. Max Lane, "Rendra Knew on Whose Side He Stood," *Inside Indonesia*, September 2010, http://www.insideindonesia.org/rendra-knew-on-whose-side-he-stood-2; Kathy Foley, "Arifin and Putu: Teater Modern Acting in New Order Indonesia," in *Intercultural Acting and Performer Training*, ed. Anuradha Kapur, Zarrilli Phillip, and T. Sasitharan (London: Routledge, 2019); Michael H. Bodden, *Resistance on the National Stage: Theater and Politics in Late New Order Indonesia* (Columbus: Ohio University Press, 2010), 22–55.

9. Fadrik Aziz Firdausi, "Sanggar seni rupa tumbuh di tengah badai Revolusi Indonesia," *tirto.id*, October 21, 2018, https://tirto.id/sanggar-seni-rupa-tumbuh-di-tengah-badai -revolusi-indonesia-c7ZD.

10. Bodden, *Resistance on the National Stage*, 132–37.

11. "Teater Kempes," *Majalah Tempo*, January 1, 1972.

12. Edwin Jurriëns, "Motion and Distortion: The Media in the Art of Jompet and Tintin," *Indonesia and the Malay World* 37, no. 109 (2009): 277–97, https://doi.org/10.1080/13639810903355224; Melê Yamomo, "Dis/Obedience Performed," *Southeast of Now: Directions in Contemporary and Modern Art in Asia* 6, no. 1 (2022): 177–81.

13. Ugoran Prasad, "Majelis and Materiality: Dramaturgy of Collective Reading," in *(Asian) Dramaturgs' Network: Sensing, Complexity, Tracing, and Doing*, ed. Charlene Rajendran and Peter Eckersall (Singapore: Centre 42, 2023), 102–9.

14. José Esteban Muñoz, *Cruising Utopia: The Then and There of Queer Futurity* (New York: NYU Press, 2009), 1–18.

Keep up to date on new scholarship

Issue alerts are a great way to stay current on all the cutting-edge scholarship from your favorite Duke University Press journals. This free service delivers tables of contents directly to your inbox, informing you of the latest groundbreaking work as soon as it is published.

To sign up for issue alerts:

1. Visit **dukeu.press/register** and register for an account. You do not need to provide a customer number.

2. After registering, visit **dukeu.press/alerts**.

3. Go to "Latest Issue Alerts" and click on "Add Alerts."

4. Select as many publications as you would like from the pop-up window and click "Add Alerts."

read.dukeupress.edu/journals